W9-AVA-139

NEW DIRECTIONS FOR TEACHING AND LEARNING

Marilla D. Svinicki, *University of Texas, Austin*
EDITOR-IN-CHIEF

R. Eugene Rice, *American Association for Higher Education*
CONSULTING EDITOR

Assessment Strategies for the On-Line Class: From Theory to Practice

Rebecca S. Anderson
University of Memphis

John F. Bauer
Towson University

Bruce W. Speck
Austin Peay State University

EDITORS

Number 91, Fall 2002

JOSSEY-BASS
San Francisco

ASSESSMENT STRATEGIES FOR THE ON-LINE CLASS: FROM THEORY TO PRACTICE
Rebecca S. Anderson, John F. Bauer, Bruce W. Speck (eds.)
New Directions for Teaching and Learning, no. 91
Marilla D. Svinicki, Editor-in-Chief
R. Eugene Rice, Consulting Editor

Microfilm copies of issues and articles are available in 16mm and 35mm, as well as microfiche in 105mm, through University Microfilms Inc., 300 North Zeeb Road, Ann Arbor, Michigan 48106-1346.

ISSN 0271-0633   electronic ISSN 1536-0768   ISBN 0-7879-6343-7

NEW DIRECTIONS FOR TEACHING AND LEARNING is part of The Jossey-Bass Higher and Adult Education Series and is published quarterly by Wiley Subscription Services, Inc., A Wiley Company, at Jossey-Bass, 989 Market Street, San Francisco, California 94103-1741. Periodicals postage paid at San Francisco, California, and at additional mailing offices. Postmaster: Send address changes to New Directions for Teaching and Learning, Jossey-Bass, 989 Market Street, San Francisco, California 94103-1741.

New Directions for Teaching and Learning is indexed in College Student Personnel Abstracts, Contents Pages in Education, and Current Index to Journals in Education (ERIC).

SUBSCRIPTIONS cost $65.00 for individuals and $130 for institutions, agencies, and libraries. Prices subject to change.

EDITORIAL CORRESPONDENCE should be sent to the editor-in-chief, Marilla D. Svinicki, The Center for Teaching Effectiveness, University of Texas at Austin, Main Building 2200, Austin, TX 78712-1111.

Cover photograph by Richard Blair/Color & Light © 1990.

www.josseybass.com

Printed in the United States of America on acid-free recycled paper containing at least 20 percent postconsumer wase.

CONTENTS

FROM THE SERIES EDITOR

About This Publication. Since 1980, *New Directions for Teaching and Learning* has brought a unique blend of theory, research, and practice to leaders in postsecondary education. We strive not only for solid substance but also for timeliness, compactness, and accessibility.

This series has the following goals:

1. To inform about current and future directions in teaching and learning in postsecondary education
2. To illuminate the context that shapes those new directions
3. To illustrate new directions through examples from real settings
4. To propose how new directions can be incorporated into still other settings

This sourcebook reflects the view that teaching deserves respect as a high form of scholarship. We believe that significant scholarship is done not only by the researcher who reports results of empirical investigations, but also by the practitioner who shares with others disciplined reflections about teaching. Contributors to this sourcebook approach questions of teaching and learning as seriously as they approach substantive questions in their own disciplines, dealing not only with pedagogical issues but also with the intellectual and social context out of which those issues arise. They deal with theory and research and with practice, and they translate from research and theory to practice and back again.

About This Volume. The chapter authors in this volume address the difficult question of evaluating the on-line work of students. With so much emphasis being placed on developing instructional material for on-line use, they argue that we must also give careful consideration to how the students' performance will be assessed. This timely set of guidelines can help instructors establish grading procedures for on-line work as rigorous as those they would apply to face-to-face work.

Marilla D. Svinicki
Editor-in-Chief
R. Eugene Rice
Consulting Editor

EDITORS' NOTES

This volume on on-line assessment might best be considered the third in a *New Directions for Teaching and Learning* trilogy involving elements of assessment and the on-line class. The first (Summer 1998) dealt with classroom assessment and the new learning paradigm. The second (Winter 2000) concerned itself with effective teaching in the on-line class. *Assessment Strategies for the On-Line Class: From Theory to Practice* is based on the premises of the two earlier works and was conceived as a continuing effort to contribute seminal material to this topical trend in higher education.

Purpose of This Volume

Internet technologies have had a profound effect on the way we conduct the business of education. Whether professors are encouraged by internal or external motivators, many are seeking information on how best to explore the realm of the digital classroom.

We began with the assumption that those in higher education who choose to go on-line with their course work need answers to at least two persistent questions: What do we need to know about grading student work in the on-line class? and What are ways we can do it? The purpose of this volume is to gather in one place a wide variety of chapters that address theoretical and practical considerations regarding the assessment of student work in the on-line classroom.

Overview of the Chapters

In Chapter One, Bruce Speck points out that professors can make informed choices about using the on-line medium by basing their instruction on pedagogical theory and evaluating two learning-teaching assessment models. He begins with a review of the brief history of on-line teaching and explains the influences of economics on educational practice.

Marshall Jones and Stephen Harmon use a question-and-answer format in Chapter Two in defining three distinct areas of assessment and identifying the tools with which to conduct the assessment.

In Chapter Three, John Bauer discusses the nature of chatrooms and bulletin boards, two popular Web site environments, and suggests a practical way that professors can apply grading rubrics to student work submitted on-line.

In Chapter Four, Robert Gray explains how professors can either "mark the screen" or use separate attachments in the grading process. He sees e-mail as the analogue of face-to-face conferencing for providing feedback.

John Nicolay tackles the issues surrounding the assessment of group projects in Chapter Five. He identifies five principles for grading the products of student collaboration and offers a cautionary note on handling plagiarism.

In Chapter Six, Jane Puckett and Rebecca Anderson caution that the movement toward on-line learning presents challenges for professional preparation programs, especially in terms of traditional field experiences. They ask if a real-world experience can be effectively monitored and assessed by the professor using the Internet.

In Chapter Seven, James Brown explores key concepts, resources, and strategies that can greatly strengthen the ability of on-line curricular offerings to accommodate learners with a wide range of disabilities.

Mark Canada in Chapter Eight argues that professors can make effective use of e-folios to enhance their students' learning and facilitate their own process of responding to student work. He maintains that e-folios have unique navigational advantages, are generally easier to maintain and share than traditional portfolios, and encourage students to develop additional communication skills.

In Chapter Nine, Michele Ford advises professors with limited technological experience to use features of their existing computer networks to communicate assessment expectations to their on-line students. E-mail and Web postings can serve this purpose.

In Chapter Ten, Joe Law, Lory Hawkes, and Christina Murphy examine the degree programs that are proliferating on-line and discuss the need to employ clearly articulated criteria for their evaluation. Such assessment efforts could begin with "Best Practices for Electronically Offered Degree and Certificate Programs," developed by the Western Interstate Commission for Higher Education.

In Chapter Eleven, Brad Mehlenbacher explains user interface and instructional design of on-line materials. He examines such criteria as accessibility, aesthetic appeal, consistency and layout, customizability and maintainability, help, and support documentation, among others.

In Chapter Twelve, Richard Bothel warns that the effectiveness of on-line assessment can be mitigated by several factors: unrealistic appraisal of the potential of on-line education, enforcement of a code of conduct, computer and telecommunication skills bias, and other limitations of on-line media.

Rebecca S. Anderson
John F. Bauer
Bruce W. Speck
Editors

REBECCA S. ANDERSON is the director of Writing Across the Curriculum for the University of Memphis, Tennessee, and an associate professor in the department of instruction and curriculum leadership.

JOHN F. BAUER is an assistant professor in the department of instructional technology at Towson University, Maryland.

BRUCE W. SPECK is professor of English and vice president for academic affairs at Austin Peay State University in Clarksville, Tennessee.

1

Professors can make informed choices about teaching in on-line classrooms by basing their instructional endeavors on pedagogical theory and evaluating two learning-teaching-assessment paradigms.

Learning-Teaching-Assessment Paradigms and the On-Line Classroom

Bruce W. Speck

The advent of the on-line classroom has provided a new opportunity for professors to consider the role of pedagogical theory by asking questions about how well students learn in virtual classrooms. Yet a review of the relatively brief history of on-line teaching shows that it has been debated more on economic than pedagogical grounds (Daniel, 1997; Feenburg, 1999; Finney, 1996; Noble, 1998a, 1998b; Taylor, 1998; Thompson, 1998), including issues of intellectual property rights (Carnevale, 2001; Chmielewski, 2000; Ellin, 2000). Perhaps the focus on economics took center stage because on-line education has been a top-down initiative in the academy and has been cast in terms of student access to education and potential enrollment gains rather than pedagogical theory. When proponents of on-line teaching do refer to pedagogical theory, they often assume that the interaction among students and between students and professor promotes active learning, or what Marchese (1997) prefers to call deep (versus surface) learning. Yet as Green (1999) notes, "Information technology has yet to transform classrooms, the instructional activities of most faculty, or the learning experiences of most students. Moreover, while we know that technology changes the learning experience, we do not have hard, consistent evidence documenting that it enhances academic achievement and learning outcomes" (p. 13). Insufficient attention to pedagogical questions and concerns arising from the practice of on-line teaching quite naturally and logically raises questions about assessment of learners in on-line classrooms.

In considering assessment, I take the position that if it is to be effective, assessment must be part and parcel of the entire learning enterprise and therefore is not a distinct stage of pedagogical theory. Assessment must be integrated into a holistic view of pedagogy. This means that any theory of assessment presumes and informs a theory of learning.

Unfortunately, professors often assess students under the authority of an inchoate theory of learning. Indeed, one of the great tragedies of American higher education is that professors are prepared by virtue of their academic training to conduct scholarship, not to teach, and yet those who elect to pursue a vocation as a college or university teacher are required to teach despite a lack of preparation to do so. Professors in the on-line classroom, although engaged in opportunities to explore teaching using new forms of technology, encounter the same question that professors in face-to-face classrooms have often chosen to sidestep: How can students be fairly and effectively assessed without a coherent theory of learning?

This chapter provides professors with information that will help them consider the need to approach assessment from a cohesive learning-teaching-assessment paradigm. To accomplish this purpose, I will first challenge the commonly held position that good teaching is based on "craft knowledge." Second, I will address what I consider to be a pressing assessment problem in all classes, but a problem that is intensified in the online class—namely, the assessment of students' writing. Third, I will discuss two major competing learning-teaching-assessment paradigms. Fourth, I will explain how the application of those paradigms would define learning and, consequently, dictate how learning should be assessed.

Challenging Craft Knowledge

Most professors operate from craft knowledge when they teach; that is, they attempt to hone their ability to teach by following the examples of teachers they believe were effective teachers, reflecting on their teaching and considering ways to improve it, and asking others involved in the craft for advice. Because many professors have not had academic training in pedagogical theory and have a low view of those who have studied pedagogy, they are skeptical about efforts to think theoretically about teaching. Such efforts are attempts, they believe, to capture what must remain existential. I encountered this attitude when I was asked to start a faculty development unit on a campus. Not long after assuming my duties, a faculty member from the College of Education said to me in a slightly sneering tone, "So, you're going to tell us how to teach." I had said nothing to provoke such a response, and I was struck by the irony of such a statement on the lips of a faculty member in education. Nevertheless, my colleague's attitude is typical of a widespread belief among professors that teaching is a craft learned chiefly through practice, including a healthy dose of trial and error. The very best teachers have a knack for teaching that is in many ways inexplicable, a position supported by some of the literature on teaching effectiveness (Beidler, 1986; Carrotte, 1999; Elbow, 1986; Epstein, 1981). Bok (1991) both articulates this point of view and calls it into question:

Because many of the greatest teachers seem to succeed spontaneously, using methods that are often peculiar to themselves, it is tempting to conclude that teaching is simply too private and personal to be improved by purposeful, organized means. But that is clearly not the case. Much teaching is ineffective or uninspired either because instructors spend too little time preparing, or because they do not know what they are doing wrong, or because they are not aware of other ways to motivate, to illuminate, and ultimately to move their students to master a body of knowledge [p. 17].

Craft knowledge—what Bok refers to as methods peculiar to a particular professor—can be valuable as an approach to understanding some aspects of teaching, but it cannot substitute for a theory of pedagogy. Indeed, craft knowledge assumes a theory of pedagogy based on intuition and experience, but does not make explicit its theoretical underpinnings, in part, because those underpinnings are grounded in individual practice and capability. Effective teaching, from a craft knowledge perspective, is frequently shrouded in mystery.

Common professorial skepticism about the possibility of and the need for pedagogical theory is buttressed by the troubling truth that experts on pedagogical theory disagree about which theoretical position should be the basis for a learning-teaching-assessment paradigm. One reason experts disagree is that learning and teaching and their assessment are extremely complex subjects. To ask questions about learning is to open Pandora's box. The questions that fly out of that box plague us.

What is learning? By *learning,* do we mean the ability to remember (and for how long?) facts, principles, ideas, or particular viewpoints so that the learner can repeat facts, principles, ideas, or particular viewpoints to some level of satisfaction for a particular professor, group of professors, or professional association? Isn't learning implicated in a tangle of issues, such as a student's particular approach to learning (learning styles), gender, age, socioeconomic background, motivation, work experience (including the number of hours a learner works while going to school), marital status, prior educational experiences, and disabilities? And aren't all those factors influenced in some way by the actual (or virtual) classroom environment, with heavy stress on a particular professor's ability to teach effectively?

What about the economics of education? Doesn't it make a difference whether learners can afford to buy books for a class (or an appropriate computer for an on-line course)? Isn't it of some importance whether an institution of higher education can offer the support needed for learners to learn, such as advising that takes account of learners' interests, economic resources for hiring and retaining professors, and classrooms designed to promote student learning (for example, classrooms that can be configured to promote cooperative learning tasks) and equipped with tools that support learning objectives?

In short, *learning* appears to be a complicated concept, and, concomitantly, the evaluation or assessment of learning appears to be equally

complex. We should not be surprised, therefore, by Terenzini's (1989) asser-
tion, "One of the most significant and imposing obstacles to the advancement of the assessment agenda at the national level is the absence of any
consensus on precisely what 'assessment' means" (p. 646). At least part of
the reason for lack of consensus at the national level is, on the one hand,
that the construct *learning* is not easily defined, and, on the other hand, that
American scholarship about teaching and learning is "mostly about teaching, and teachers" (Marchese, 1997, p. 8), not about learning. The obstacles
at the national level are no less acute at the local classroom level.
(Mehlenbacher provides additional insights into how to describe learners in
Chapter Eleven.)

The knotty problem of significant disagreement among experts about
what learning is and how learning should be assessed fuels professors'
adherence to craft knowledge for two reasons. First, debates about learning
can be technical discussions that require a good deal of knowledge. To
develop the knowledge base necessary to follow those discussions requires
time that many professors simply do not feel they have, given their other
responsibilities. Second, professors overestimate their teaching success and
therefore believe that their craft knowledge works well enough both to
enable them to be good teachers and to improve. For instance, Cross
(1977), in reporting her research on teaching at one university, found that
professors believe they are excellent teachers. Of the professors she sur-
veyed, "An amazing 94 percent rate themselves as above-average teachers,
and 68 percent rank themselves in the top quarter on teaching performance" (p. 10). Craft knowledge appears to support the professorial contention, "I don't know pedagogical theory, and I'm doing a good job as a
teacher, so why do I need to study pedagogy?"

Pressing the Need for a Cohesive Paradigm in the Assessment of Writing

Because writing is the major, and perhaps only, means of communication in
an on-line classroom, issues related to the evaluation of writing should pre-
occupy any discussion of how professors evaluate student performance in
the virtual classroom. (Gray, in Chapter Four, stresses this same point.)
Indeed, the oral nature of face-to-face instruction is replaced by writing for
both professors and students. Certainly, on-line students have other ways to
communicate with professors, including telephone conversations and face-
to-face conferences when students are geographically proximate to professors. However, the intention of the on-line classroom is to foster
professor-student and student-student communication by writing, whether
that writing is used to communicate in chatrooms, on bulletin boards, in
e-mail, through instructions that point to other written documents (links
that lead students to particular URLs with written text), and by written drafts
and presentation copies students submit to fulfill assignment requirements.

Among most professors, lack of understanding a full-fledged theory of writing pedagogy is not only a hindrance to effective evaluation of writing but also an opportunity for craft knowledge to go awry. When professors evaluate writing without recourse to the fruits of composition theory, they often fall prey to practices that actually have a negative impact on students' ability to write effectively. However, even if professors did investigate the literature on assessing writing, they would find that experts disagree about how writing should be evaluated (Speck, 1998a, 1998b; Speck and Jones, 1998; White, Lutz, and Kamusikiri, 1996; Zak and Weaver, 1998). The nature of that disagreement can be divided into two competing learning-teaching-assessment paradigms that are quite different from each other. In essence, professors may choose between the two paradigms, and that choice will define the nature of both writing and assessment.

Writing is particularly important when we assess student learning because good writing requires the use of skills that exemplify effective communication. As Elsbree (1985) affirms, "At its best, composition is a corporate activity involving fellow readers, writers, and teachers. Sharing views, experiences, or research with others and submitting them for criticism, discussion, and modification are essential parts of the process of effective communication" (pp. 23–24). Zinsser (1988) goes so far as to say that the teaching of writing should be a community effort by all teachers. He notes that English teachers "shouldn't have to assume the whole responsibility for imparting a skill that's basic to every area of life. That should be everybody's job. That's citizenship" (p. 13). Elsbree and Zinsser affirm the importance of writing not only as a means of learning in all the academic disciplines, but also as a lifelong skill that promotes citizenship in a democratic society. The premier position that writing holds in the academy and in society is intensified in the on-line classroom, where writing is the dominant mode of communication among students and teachers, so dominant, in fact, that it replaces oral communication. When we also realize that writing is a powerful way for students to demonstrate their learning, our interest in evaluating that writing should be piqued.

Unfortunately, when we investigate the literature on writing assessment (Speck, 1998a), we find disputed grounds for assessing written products, including debates about the relationship between the process professors can use to teach students how to write and the evaluation of products that issue from that process, questions about the terminology professors use to describe evaluation (*grading, marking, assessing, evaluating*), and political, cultural, and ethical concerns about how writing is evaluated (Speck, 2000). Theoretical presuppositions about evaluation complicate the disputed grounds for assessment because a particular theoretical position is enmeshed with issues related to reliability, validity, fairness, and professional judgment.

Writing theorists engaged in debates about assessing writing quickly recognize that on a continuum of theoretical positions about writing assessment, two are prominent. One claims that writing can be assessed by using various testing measures based on psychometric principles. Standardized tests of writing are examples of that approach. The other claims that local measures of evaluation based on what is being taught and learned in a particular classroom are the best, perhaps only, successful way to evaluate writing. Portfolio assessment represents one way adherents of this approach would promote what they call authentic assessments. (In Chapter Eight, Canada discusses authentic assessment of portfolios.) These two approaches to evaluating writing are based on two paradigms of assessment, two theoretical positions, each grounded in very different assumptions about learning, so it is appropriate to explain briefly these two learning-teaching-assessment paradigms before raising issues related to the application of those paradigms in the on-line classroom.

Competing Learning-Teaching-Assessment Paradigms

Anderson (1998) provides a critique of the two major competing paradigms—one she labels Traditional and the other as Alternative—and using nine points of reference, compares their philosophical beliefs and theoretical assumptions. For instance, Traditional assessment assumes that the purpose of evaluation is to document learning. Students are seen as the recipients of knowledge, so their function is to absorb a body of information and demonstrate that they have absorbed that knowledge by answering test questions correctly.

The notion that students are recipients of knowledge has been labeled passive or surface learning (as opposed to active or deep learning), and the means of delivering knowledge—predominantly the lecture method (McKeachie, 1999; O'Donnell and Dansereau, 1994)—reinforces the criticism of the Traditional approach that students are indeed quite passive as learners and engage predominantly in surface learning (Biggs, 1996; O'Donnell and Dansereau, 1992). Thus, a major criticism of the focus on surface learning, which is promoted by Traditional assessment methods, is that it does not allow for higher-level thinking skills: synthesis, analysis, and evaluation.

One reason adherents of the Alternative camp question the ability of Traditional assessment methods to capture and evaluate higher-order thinking skills is that the result of students' application of such skills cannot be measured adequately using Traditional assessment measures. Why is this? The application of higher-order skills, the Alternative camp insists, does not result in uniform results. For instance, if a professor asks students to evaluate the Clinton presidency in terms of the effectiveness of foreign policy decisions enacted by the former president, the result of such an analysis, even given "objective" indicators, undoubtedly would elicit a variety of plausible responses. (Even experts on the Clintonian presidency would undoubtedly disagree about the effectiveness of foreign policy decisions.) However, the assessment measures championed by the Traditional approach, called norm-referenced tests, assume that the scores for a test will follow a bell curve. "Norm referencing," as White (1985) points out, "assumes a normal distribution of the skills it measures" (p. 64).

In other words, norm-referenced tests stress one right answer for each test question and are based on the assumption that students' learning can be rank-ordered. A few students will answer most of the test questions correctly, and a few will answer most of the test questions incorrectly. Most of the remaining students' answers will be distributed between these two extremes.

What role, then, would a norm-referenced test play in assessing students' evaluations of Clintonian foreign policy? Such a test would require students to think about Clinton's foreign policy in fairly prescribed ways because the assessment of their thinking, their learning, would focus on what are viewed as the right answers. Traditional assessment methods therefore define learning in terms of right and wrong answers. Students are receptacles for right answers. Learning is being able to identify the correct answer for a test question. Thus, evaluation of learning is considered objective in that correct answers, if tests are valid and reliable, are indisputably correct. Learning, it appears, can be standardized, and test scores can determine to what extent a student has learned.

Those who champion the Alternative approach take a different approach to assessment, preferring criterion-referenced tests, which are locally developed and based on test outcomes for a particular classroom setting. Whereas those in the Traditional camp appear to decontextualize learning by focusing on the science of test development without much concern for the learning environment, those in the Alternative camp put heavy stress on the classroom context. Learning, for the Alternative camp, is inextricably linked with the conditions in which learning takes place, and no norm-referenced test can possibly take into account adequately multiple learning situations, for both individual students and students in particular classrooms. As Jones and Harmon note in Chapter Two, "Decisions about assessment are relative to particular circumstances and experience levels."

Under the Alternative approach, students are not seen as receptacles of knowledge; rather, they are inquirers. As Fosnot (1991) says, "Learning needs to be conceived as something a learner does, not something that is done *to* a learner" (p. 5). Learning is a natural condition of life, and proponents of the Alternative approach seek to nurture the process of learning so that students can explore issues and seek to understand how to make meaning out of complex phenomena. Thus, students are extremely active in the process of learning and are both encouraged and enabled to go beyond surface answers by using higher-level thinking skills of synthesis, analysis, and evaluation. In fact, learning requires social engagement with others to the extent that students collaborate in their learning, something that the Traditional approach frowns on because collaboration muddies the assessment waters of norm-referenced tests, which are designed to test individuals.

In fact, proponents of the Alternative approach stress the need for evaluators to admit that evaluation is never objective because it takes place in a social context framed by political concerns. Thus, test scores, grades, and other assessment results are inherently biased and subjective. This is not to say that the Alternative approach eschews attempts to pinpoint and minimize destructive biases, but the claim that tests can be objective seems overstated from the perspective of the Alternative approach.

Without discussing every thrust and parry of these two camps as they engage in pedagogical, philosophical, and rhetorical repartee, I think professors can see that two very different belief systems concerning the definition and evaluation of student learning are locked in mortal combat. The combatants in this contest are engaged in battle because assessment issues are of great consequence, and any resolution of the conflict will have a wide-reaching impact on policies regarding what learning-teaching-assessment paradigm will be used to define learning, inform the preparation of teachers, and chart the course for pedagogical theory.

Evaluating and Assessing Learning in the On-line Classroom

Each paradigm, as I have shown, is based on particular assumptions about learning and the assessment of learning. In what follows, I raise issues related to the application of both the Traditional and Alternative paradigms to the on-line classroom.

The Traditional Paradigm. Setting aside questions about what constitutes effective teaching, what roles race and gender play in test construction, and what impact learning styles have in students' understanding of facts and concepts the professor presents, among other questions that impinge on teaching and learning, I question the supposed ability of a mathematical-scientific approach to evaluate the highly complex behavior of learning and writing. This is not to deny that attempts have been made to evaluate writing on objective measures, such as T-unit analysis (Dixon, 1972; Witte, 1983) and computer analysis (Breland, 1996). But even Breland (1996), a proponent of using computer technology to evaluate writing, admits that the data generated by statistical analyses do not support the claim that computers can grade essays. In fact, Breland affirms that "grading seems an unlikely task for the computer," noting that computers "can help students prepare and edit written work, and they can help teachers by providing information about the students' writing that the teachers may have overlooked. Such information, however, needs to be mediated by human judgment" (p. 255). In fact, whether computers can help students *edit* their writing certainly depends on how *editing* is defined, and I suspect that those who take Breland's position have a mechanical and simplistic concept of editing that does not do justice to the social nuances necessary for effective editing (Speck, 1991, 1992).

The interplay between statistical analysis and human judgment is extremely complex, but those in the Traditional camp tend to argue that statistical analyses provide data with predictive power, the power to foretell student success. Indeed, parents, students, and legislators may find such an argument appealing, believing that the data generated by such an approach are adequate proof of writing quality or ability. As White (1996) notes, speaking of shareholders outside the academy, "They want normative numbers, success rates of groups, and ways of identifying failing students and incompetent teachers" (p. 301). Indeed, students "want consistent measures that are determined not by teacher subjectivity but by clear standards" (pp. 301–302). The Traditional approach appears to cut through subjectivity by providing data that not only place students in rank order according to ability but also predict student success in future writing endeavors. In a culture dominated by science and the prestige associated with the scientific method, the Traditional approach can be quite appealing. Not incidentally, a major concern of the Traditional approach for on-line classrooms will be test security, presumably because individual test scores are important indicators of what individuals learned.

However, an on-line class based on the Traditional method may unduly limit professional judgment. First, the statistical procedures plied by its proponents are foreign to most professors. In essence, professors would be asked to trust a method that they cannot articulate, deferring judgment to instruments developed by psychometricians. Second, such deferral of judgment would require in large part assessment that focuses on countable features of writing or objective measures, such as format, grammar, mechanics, spelling, sentence length, paragraph length, placement of topic sentences, number of pages, frequency of passive (or active) voice, number of times technical terms are or are not used, and so forth. Any combination of such measures would somehow add up to an assessment of written products, sans professorial judgment. The problem, of course, is that these measures do not appear to tell us much about communication effectiveness (Hirsch and Harrington, 1981). Students can write a paper that is impeccably correct—and vacuous.

An even greater problem is that the Traditional method appears to promote rote exercises, generally at the sentence level, that provide negligible insight into how to teach students to write. Such an approach to writing pedagogy is inimical to research that supports the writing process as an act of invention characterized by fits and starts (Elbow, 1981; Flower and Hayes, 1981; Murray, 1991). The absence of clear connections between the Traditional method and the writing process raises troubling questions about the ways the Traditional method would help students satisfy objective criteria of writing ability.

For instance, if fluency, that is, the length of a response in a chatroom, is the basis for assessing students' responses, then a student who writes prolix responses will get higher grades than a student who does not. Fluency, however, is not a lone measure for assessing writing. Generally, professors are concerned about evaluating the content of a piece of writing, but content, for a piece of writing that is produced at the moment, at the point of utterance, such as many chatroom responses, should take into account the element of spontaneity. That element not only may defy assessment but also confound it by allowing the kinds of errors that attend spontaneity, thus challenging measures of correctness embedded in the Traditional approach. (For insights into assessing students' writing in chatrooms, see Chapter Three.)

Theoretically, the problem of the fit between methods issued by the Traditional approach and research that supports the process approach to composition remains a major issue when assessment of writing is under discussion. Indeed, questions about the relationship between summative assessment—the raison d'être of the Traditional approach—and formative assessment, which is embedded in the concept of the writing process, largely remain unanswered, most likely because the Traditional approach is not designed to address the nuances of formative assessment. Therefore, to design an on-line classroom given the focus of the Traditional approach requires much attention to final written products, which will have to be evaluated on highly objective measures. Student learning will most likely be gauged by canons of correctness related to surface features of students' writing: spelling, mechanics, and grammar. But because such canons are obviously insufficient to determine what else students may or may not have learned about how to write effectively, subjective measures, perhaps in the guise of objective measures, will be used to evaluate organization, quality of ideas, and effective use of evidence to persuade targeted audiences. Thus, even the Traditional approach, because it does not have the power necessary to assess student learning as demonstrated in student writing, will call on professors' subjective judgments, unless writing, as a way to demonstrate learning, is reduced to right answers. This possibility, when realized, vitiates the nature of writing.

The Alternative Paradigm. The Alternative paradigm understands learning as a process in which students have opportunities to explore ideas and make mistakes. In fact, mistakes can be seen as growth in learning because learning entails feeling along one's way, often in the dark. Just as inventors often follow numerous blind alleys before hitting on a useful discovery, so student learning depends on the freedom to investigate ideas that may lead to dead ends. Learning, however, is not merely a matter of individual effort in groping toward light; rather, it is a social phenomenon because language is social in nature, and without language, learning is severely limited, perhaps impossible. Thus, students can learn from each other, and professors can learn from students through the written language.

The on-line classroom informed by the Alternative paradigm will be structured so that students have freedom in making decisions about their learning. For instance, they will be able to select topics for research that inter-est them. They will not be seen as empty vessels or vessels with empty or near empty chambers marked "physics," "history," "philosophy," and so forth that need to be filled by the professor's knowledgeable, flowing voice. Rather, stu-dents will be seen as capable of learning and responsible for their own learn-ing. When students do not want to take responsibility for their own learning, professors will recognize that much of students' failure to take responsibility is due to an educational system that has asked students to find the right answers for the test questions. Thus, professors will continue to insist on the need for students to act responsibly as learners.

An on-line classroom based on the Alternative paradigm will subscribe to the writing process, and professors in such classrooms will design assignments that allow for interplay between process and product, between formative and summative assessment. Professors will teach students how to approach various sorts of writing tasks and will make explicit at the outset what the criteria are for success in completing a particular task. In fact, pro-fessors will enlist students to help develop criteria for evaluating writing assignments, whether chatroom discussions, bulletin board postings, or a variety of other writing assignments.

While making as explicit as possible the evaluative relationship between the process of writing and the products that issue from that pro-cess, the professor who subscribes to the Alternative paradigm will acknowl-edge that professorial judgment is still a valid part of the evaluation process. What the professor can make explicit in evaluative decisions, he or she will make explicit, but the professor also will uphold the premise that assess-ment cannot be reduced to objective criteria. Human judgment, both the judgment of students and the professor, will have value in an on-line class grounded in the Alternative paradigm, and grades will continue to be con-tested because the professor will not take the position that because he or she is the "professional" in the classroom, his or her judgment is infallible. Nevertheless, the professor, quite realistically, will recognize that grades are required in the existing system of higher education and will strive to be as fair as possible in grading while allowing assessment to serve grades, not grades assessment.

Conclusion

Clearly, I have shown that my choice concerning which learning-teaching-evaluation paradigm better suits the on-line classroom is the Alternative approach. I make this choice because writing is warp and woof of the virtual classroom, and I am extremely skeptical that the Traditional paradigm, at least as it has been used historically, will offer much help in assessing writ-ing effectively because the paradigm defines learning inappropriately. Unfortunately, the Traditional paradigm has powerful supporters, especially considering the huge economic investment in and return on norm-referenced tests, such as the Scholastic Aptitude Test. In addition, the publics outside the academy are generally quite convinced that the Traditional paradigm tells them the truth about assessment. Norm-referenced tests have become an institution, and much of their power lies in our culture's deep-seated belief that numbers tell the Truth and that students should be rank-ordered.

Such an approach to learning, teaching, and assessment, from my perspective as a professor of writing, is wrong-headed. Writing should be defined as a process that leads to a product, and the relationship between process and product is so intimate that it cannot be separated. How students learn to write in on-line classrooms, as in other classrooms, is wed to what students write to show that they are learning. The literature on the writing process gives clear guidance on how to teach writing so that it can be a tool for self-discovery, for learning. The literature on writing assessment, if read from the perspective of the Alternative paradigm, also gives clear guidance on ways that teachers across the curriculum, including teachers in the on-line classroom, can nurture and support the writing process so that students join professors in evaluating student writing. If professors of on-line classes fail to heed the expert opinion of those who have provided ample evidence that the process approach to teaching writing and the use of formative and summative assessments of writing support each other, then on-line classrooms will fail to serve students in the same ways that face-to-face classrooms have failed to serve students. If that happens, the promise of technology to promote student learning will be unfulfilled, the potential of technology to serve learning will have been squandered, and students will have reason to reinforce their mistaken belief that education is defined as the attainment of a degree, virtual or otherwise.

References

Anderson, R. S. "Why Talk About Different Ways to Grade? The Shift from Traditional Assessment to Alternative Assessment." In R. S. Anderson and B. W. Speck (eds.), *Changing the Way We Grade Student Performance: Classroom Assessment and the New Learning Paradigm.* New Directions for Teaching and Learning, no. 74. San Francisco: Jossey-Bass, 1998.

Beidler, P. G. (ed.). *Distinguished Teachers on Effective Teaching.* New Directions for Teaching and Learning, no. 28. San Francisco: Jossey-Bass, 1986.

Biggs, J. "Enhancing Teaching Through Constructive Alignment." *Higher Education,* 1996, *32,* 347–364.

Bok, D. *The Importance of Teaching.* New York: American Council of Learned Societies, 1991.

Breland, H. M. "Computer-Assisted Writing Assessment: The Politics of Sciences Versus the Humanities. In E. M. White, W. D. Lutz, and S. Kamusikiri (eds.), *Assessment of Writing: Politics, Policies, Practices.* New York: Modern Language Association of America, 1996.

Carnevale, D. "University of Vermont Considers Intellectual-Property Policy to Foster Distance Education." *Chronicle of Higher Education,* June 8, 2001, p. A34.

Carrotte, P. "Turning Academics into Teachers." *Teaching in Higher Education,* 1999, *4,* 411–413.

Chmielewski, C. M. "Protecting Your Intellectual Property Rights On-Line." *NEA Today,* 2000, *19*(2), 20.

Cross, K. P. (1977). "Not *Can* But *Will* College Teaching Be Improved?" In J. A. Centra (ed.), *Renewing and Evaluating Teaching.* New Directions for Higher Education, no. 17. San Francisco: Jossey-Bass.

Daniel, J. S. "Why Universities Need Technology Strategies." *Change,* 1997, *29*(4), 11–17.

Dixon, E. A. (1972). "Syntactic Indexes and Student Writing Performance." *Elementary English, 49*(5), 714–716.

Elbow, P. *Writing with Power: Techniques for Mastering the Writing Process.* New York: Oxford University Press, 1981.

Elbow, P. *Embracing Contraries: Explorations in Teaching and Learning.* New York: Oxford University Press, 1986.

Ellin, A. "The Battle in Cyberspace: Universities and Professors Debate Ownership of Materials on the Web." *New York Times,* Aug. 6, 2000, p. ED15.

Elsbree, L. "Learning to Write Through Mutual Coaching." In J. Katz (ed.), *Teaching as Though Students Mattered.* New Directions for Teaching and Learning, no. 21. San Francisco: Jossey-Bass, 1985.

Epstein, J. (ed.). *Masters: Portraits of Great Teachers.* New York: Basic Books, 1981.

Feenberg, A. "Distance Learning: Promise or Threat?" [http://www.rohan.sdsu.edu/faculty/feenberg/TELE3.htm]. 1999.

Finney, J. E. (1996). "An Interview: Michael A. Leavitt." *Crosstalk,* 4(2), 2–3.

Flower, L., and Hayes, J. R. "A Cognitive Process Theory of Writing." *College Composition and Communication,* 1981, *32,* 365–387.

Fosnot, C. T. *Enquiring Teachers, Enquiring Learners: A Constructivist Approach for Teaching.* New York: Teachers College Press, 1991.

Green, K. C. "When Wishes Come True: Colleges and the Convergence of Access, Lifelong Learning, and Technology." *Change,* 1999, *31*(2), 11–15.

Hirsch, E. D., and Harrington, D. P. "Measuring the Communicative Effectiveness of Prose." In C. H. Frederiksen and J. F. Dominic (eds.), *Writing: The Nature, Development, and Teaching of Written Communication.* Mahwah, N.J.: Erlbaum, 1981.

Marchese, T. J. "The New Conversations About Learning: Insights from Neuroscience and Anthropology, Cognitive Science and Work-Place Studies." In B. Cambridge (ed.), *Assessing Impact: Evidence and Action.* Washington, D.C.: American Association for Higher Education, 1997.

McKeachie, W. J. *Teaching Tips: Strategies, Research, and Theory for College and University Teachers.* (10th ed.) Boston: Houghton Mifflin, 1999.

Murray, D. M. (1991). *The Craft of Revision.* Forth Worth, Tex.: Holt, Rinehart, and Winston, 1991.

Noble, D. F. "Digital Diploma Mills: The Automation of Higher Education." *First Monday.* [http://www.firstmonday.dk/issues/issue3_1/noble/]. 1998a.

Noble, D. F. "Digital Diploma Mills: Part II: The Coming Battle over On-Line Instruction." [http://www.uwo.ca/uwofa/articles/di_dip_2.html]. 1998b.

O'Donnell, A. M., and Dansereau, D. F. "Scripted Cooperation in Student Dyads: A Method for Analyzing and Enhancing Academic Learning and Performance." In R. Hertz-Lazarowitz and N. Miller (eds.), *Instruction in Cooperative Groups: The Theoretical Anatomy of Group Learning.* New York: Cambridge University Press, 1992.

O'Donnell, A., and Dansereau, D. F. "Learning from Lectures: Effects of Cooperative Review." *Journal of Experimental Education,* 1994, *61*(2), 116–125.

Speck, B. W. "Editorial Authority in the Author-Editor Relationship." *Technical Communication,* 1991, *38*(3), 300–315.

Speck, B. W. "The Professional Writing Teacher as Author's Editor." *Technical Communication Quarterly,* 1992, *1*(3), 37–57.

Speck, B. W. *Grading Students' Writing: An Annotated Bibliography.* Westport, Conn.: Greenwood Press, 1998a.

Speck, B. W. "Unveiling Some of the Mystery of Professional Judgment in Classroom Assessment." In R. S. Anderson and B. W. Speck (eds.), *Changing the Way We Grade Student Performance: Classroom Assessment and the New Learning Paradigm.* New Directions for Teaching and Learning, no. 74. San Francisco: Jossey-Bass, 1998b.

Speck, B. W. *Grading Students' Classroom Writing: Issues and Strategies.* Washington, D.C.: George Washington University, Graduate School of Education and Human Development, 2000.

Speck, B. W., and Jones, T. R. "Direction in the Grading of Writing? What the Literature on the Grading of Writing Does and Doesn't Tell Us." In F. Zak and C. C. Weaver (eds.), *The Theory and Practice of Grading: Problems and Possibilities.* Albany: State University of New York Press, 1998.

Taylor, K. S. "Higher Education: From Craft-Production to Capitalist Enterprise?" *First Monday.* [http://www.firstmonday.dk/issues/issue3_9/taylor/index.html]. 1998.

Terenzini, P. T. "Assessment with Open Eyes: Pitfalls in Studying Student Outcomes." *Journal of Higher Education,* 1989, *60*(6), 644–664.

Thompson, T. H. "Three Futures of the Electronic University: To Dream the Possible Dream." *Educom Review,* 1998, *33*(2), 1–9. [http://www.educause./edu/pub/er. review.reviewArticles.33234.html].

White, E. M. *Teaching and Assessing Writing.* San Francisco: Jossey-Bass, 1985.

White, E. M. "Response: Assessment as a Site of Contention." In E. M. White, W. D. Lutz, and S. Kamusikiri (eds.), *Assessment of Writing: Politics, Policies, Practices.* New York: Modern Language Association of America, 1996.

White, E. M., Lutz, W. D., and Kamusikiri, S. (eds.). *Assessment of Writing: Politics, Policies, Practices.* New York: Modern Language Association of America, 1996.

Witte, S. P. "Topical Structure and Writing Quality: Some Possible Text-Based Explanations for Readers' Judgments of Student Writing." *Visible Language,* 1983, *12*(2), 177–205.

Zak, F., and Weaver, C. C. (eds.). *The Theory and Practice of Grading Writing: Problems and Possibilities.* Albany: State University of New York Press, 1998.

Zinsser, W. *Writing to Learn.* New York: HarperCollins, 1988.

BRUCE W. SPECK is professor of English and vice president for academic affairs at Austin Peay State University in Clarksville, Tennessee.

2

Universities around the world are offering classes on the Internet. This chapter answers questions about the nature of on-line courses and how assessment is done in these courses to help faculty understand how on-line learning can enhance student learning.

What Professors Need to Know About Technology to Assess On-Line Student Learning

Marshall G. Jones, Stephen W. Harmon

The title of this chapter is phrased as a statement. It perhaps would be more accurate to phrase it as a question: "What *Do* Professors Need to Know About Technology to Assess On-Line Student Learning?" We prefer to think of it as a question for two reasons. The first is that the implementation of Web-based instruction (WBI) and the science and art of assessment are evolving daily, which makes definitive statements difficult. The second is that the use of WBI and decisions about assessment are relative to particular circumstances and experience levels. In previous publications, we have explained this in terms of levels of WBI (Harmon and Jones, 1999) and considered the systemic nature of the implementation of WBI in various environments (Jones, Harmon, and Lowther, 2002; Jones and Harmon, 2002). In this chapter, we do not propose a theory so much as we seek to answer some of the most common questions related to the intersection of technology and assessment as it relates to WBI.

The chapter is organized in a straightforward question-and-answer format to address issues of assessment in WBI. In order to do this, we believe it is necessary to define assessment related to the questions. Our definition is based on the definitions and domains of our discipline, instructional design and technology (Seels and Richey, 1994) and the unique nature of WBI (President's Committee of Advisors on Science and Technology, 1997). In the discipline of instructional technology, we define three distinct areas of assessment: to monitor student progress, promote learning, and evaluate the effectiveness of the course. Any type of assessment must define a vision

NEW DIRECTIONS FOR TEACHING AND LEARNING, no. 91, Fall 2002   © Wiley Periodicals, Inc.

for what assessment is to do (Niguidula, 1997; Branzburg, 2001) and then decide on what tools to use to conduct the assessment. The tools in WBI can be similar to those used to assess learning in traditional classrooms in intent but may differ in implementation. We address various tools within our three areas of assessment to help provide operational definitions of the tools and suggestions for how to use the tools within an on-line course. But before we get to these discussions, a brief overview of how an on-line course works is in order.

How an On-Line Course Works

On-line courses are distance education courses that take place in a computer-mediated environment and use software and functionality available through the Internet. These courses typically take place in a course management system. Three of the most common course management systems are Blackboard's CourseInfo (http://www.courseinfo.com), WebCT (http://Webct.com), and eCollege (http://ecollege.com). Course management systems provide a secure password-protected environment in which students may work on course materials within a curriculum. These environments provide tracking and data collection capabilities of registered users in the course. Professors typically have little responsibility for the technical workings of these environments; rather, they administer the course from three common areas within a course management system: communication, information presentation, and instructional management. Each area provides opportunities and challenges to the professor.

Our definition of an on-line course assumes a high degree of interaction among the students and between the instructor and the students (Harmon and Jones, 1999). The conception many people have of such courses is one where students enter the course management system, read from prepared lessons, usually in the form of text, study content, and then take tests. It is quite similar to correspondence courses. Our position is that on-line students are better served by greater communication and interaction with their class peers and their professors.

Common Challenges and Questions for Professors New to On-Line Classes

Q: Do I need to know how to write Web pages to teach an on-line course?

A: Yes and no. Technically it is not required. In many systems, you can post course content in the form of word-processed documents, PowerPoint presentations, digital images, digital audio, or digital video files without any knowledge of how to write a Web page. However Web-based courses exist in HTML (Hyper Text Markup Language, the code used to write Web pages), and at some point you will find a need to know at least a little bit about it. Software packages such as Microsoft's Front Page and Macromedia's

Dreamweaver make writing pages possible without knowing code, but the software is easier to understand if you take the time to develop a rudimentary understanding of HTML. In short, to get started, you likely do not need to know anything about HTML, but as you work, you will want to learn some basics.

Q: What kind of technical skills do I need to create an on-line course?

A: Beyond the ability to work with your computer, not many. Course management systems provide most of the functionality you will need. You will need to learn how to use the course management system, but typically this is no more difficult than learning to use any other piece of basic software. Most universities provide training and technical support to faculty who are creating courses on-line. New course management systems are providing the ability to communicate verbally in real time, but most systems still rely on the transmission of text, so you may need good typing skills and speed. If you choose to post media files, such as pictures, video, or audio, you will need the skills to find or create and edit them, or you will need access to someone who has these skills. You are unlikely ever to learn all the skills you need to know at one time; things change too much and too quickly. What you hope to do is to build up a level of proficiency and comfort that will allow you to find the answers to particular questions as they arise.

Assessment Used to Monitor Student Progress

By taking measurements of what a student has learned or, perhaps more accurately, what a student is able to do at some defined point in a course, the instructor can determine where that student stands in relationship to the body of knowledge to be covered, and the learner can determine where he or she stands with respect to the instructor's intentions. This type of evaluation is often summative in nature and may occur at the end of an instructional unit or class. The best examples of this may be the midterm and the final exam and the ubiquitous research paper. These types of progress indicators in a face-to-face class can then be used to allow the instructor to suggest remediation to a student or perhaps to provide access to more advanced material for some learners. On-line assessment can provide for these tools as well.

Common Questions About Tests and Exams in an On-Line Course.

Q: What kind of questions can I ask in an on-line course exam?

A: It depends on the system, but most systems that provide testing features support two types of questions: those that can be graded by the computer and those that the instructor must grade. Automated grading ability questions are things like multiple choice, true or false, or matching items that cover didactic content and have a single right answer that you set when you write the question. The system can then grade the questions, return feedback to the student, and record the score automatically in an individual student's records. You can ask essay questions and short-answer questions as well. More sophisticated systems provide some ability to parse short-answer questions, and cutting-edge systems provide a capability to analyze essay questions (Macklin, Harmon, Jones, and Evans, 2002), options that usually require that you read the questions and grade them manually. The grade is typically entered in the management system, and registered students can log in and see their scores and your feedback once you have graded their work. In some cases, the university's record system is connected to the course system, thus making all phases of the course, from registration to final grading, connected. Integrated systems such as these are often referred to as portal systems.

Q: Can people cheat on these tests or exams?

A: You bet. If they are taking the class at a distance, it is possible for a student to have someone else take the exam or use notes or other sources without your knowledge. To guard against this, most systems allow a student to access the exam only one time and allow the professor to set up a time limit for the exam. Some universities set up exam centers with computers and a proctor, which requires students to come to a central location, with proper identification, to take the exam. This option has the drawback of negating many of the benefits of on-line education by requiring students to travel to a specific location. One option is to develop assessments that are more performance based than exam based. To this end, many on-line professors rely on term or research papers to monitor student progress.

More sophisticated approaches to preventing cheating are under development. One approach is to require students to fill out an extensive questionnaire of personal information at the beginning of the term. It would consist of a hundred or so questions that would be common knowledge to the student but would be unlikely to be known by anyone else (for example, Where were you born? What is your favorite color?). The system would store these questions and their answers in a database and choose a random sample of them to ask the student before he or she was allowed to take the exam. If a student did not get all answers correct, the system would assume that someone other than the student was taking the exam and not allow the student to proceed. The most sophisticated work is being done in biometrics. It is now possible to obtain relatively inexpensive biometric scanners, such as retinal pattern, finger or palm print, or voice print, and attach them to home computers. The student must pass the biometric scan before being allowed to take the exam. Of course, neither of these approaches ensures that someone is not sitting next to the student helping him or her with the answers. For that reason, as well as pedagogical efficacy, we recommend using more authentic assessment techniques whenever possible.

Q: Can students submit assignments by e-mail?

A: Yes, but depending on the e-mail server, the size of the attached files may cause problems with the mail system. Short word-processed papers should not cause problems with any mail server, but submissions of large media files could be a problem. The most common one is that your mailbox will fill up with student assignments, thus effectively shutting your account down. The academic computing center can provide information on the amount of space allowed for e-mail. For example, if a mail system provides 20 megabytes of space and the average size of the assignment that students send is 200 kilobytes, one hundred student assignments will fit in the mail system.

A useful alternative is a digital drop box, which most course management systems have, for students to post assignments in the course system. The advantages of these over e-mail are many. First, you are not mixing your class sections in your e-mail account or mixing class-related e-mail with your regular e-mail account. Second, most drop boxes record the day and time a student posts an assignment and can connect the assignment to a student's individual record. This means that once you grade the paper, the grade is immediately transmitted to the student. Furthermore, you can set the system up to stop allowing assignments after a particular date and time, thus helping you deal with keeping track of late assignments.

Q: What format should students submit their assignments in?

A: For papers, rich text format (.rtf) is best; it is nearly universally compatible with all word processing packages. If documents are saved in this format it does not matter if they are written on a PC or a Mac or in Microsoft Works or Appleworks. Text (.txt) files are also universal but fail to preserve the formatting of papers. For other media files, the format depends on the needs of the class and the requirements of the project. Obviously, you will need to make sure that you can open the files your students are sending. Because so many different types of software are available, you are bound to run into the problem of conflicting software versions or having students submit projects using software that you do not own. Be prepared to address this issue. We recommend specifying the software and version number you want the assignment done in (for example, PowerPoint for Office 2000).

Q: Isn't it easy to plagiarize a paper?

A: Technically yes, though it may depend on the topic of the paper. Places on the Internet such as http://schoolsucks.com provide term papers on a wide variety of topics, though they generally center around the general education requirements. Specialty topics are available but often expensive. But plagiarism is relatively easy to monitor. Although most faculty would be hard-pressed to check the references of every student's papers, on-line search capabilities allow rapid checking of papers from your office desk.

Several sophisticated tools, such as the Glatt Plagiarism Screening Program (http://www.plagiarism.com), detect plagiarism. Others, such as Integriguard (http://www.integriguard.com/), allow you to copy paragraphs from a paper and paste them into the tool search window, and the tool's search engine then looks for that paragraph on the Web. We have had good luck detecting plagiarism using the Google search engine (http://www.google.com) by entering unusual phrases from the paper in question. The search engine returns locations where these phrases may be found on the Internet.

These systems are powerful though certainly not foolproof. A creative plagiarizer who invests a lot of time and energy into the craft can certainly beat the system. This can be very hard work, and it might be argued that most people who plagiarize don't do it because they want to work *harder*.

Q: What others ways can I assess student learning in an on-line class?

A: Student projects and portfolios are proven ways to assess student learning. When a class exists in a digital or electronic environment, it seems logical to require electronic or Web-based portfolios, though what you require will obviously depend on the needs of the class and the purpose of the assessment. Also consider the skill level of the students and the resources required to support an assessment activity.

Most of our students bring to the class either Web development skills or technical skills that make it possible for them to learn Web development skills within the context of the class. Students may need support in terms of technical assistance, server space, and specialized hardware and software to create Web-based products as projects. Where students get this support may vary. In on-line degree programs, these skills may be course prerequisites. If students do not bring these skills with them, you or your institution will need to provide support for students—perhaps references or tutorials. Visibooks (www.visibooks.com) provides good free books on learning Web development software such as Microsoft's Front Page and Macromedia's Dreamweaver. Or course or lab assistants may be available to help students on highly technical problems. In past classes, we have had alumni of our on-line courses come back and work as teaching assistants.

Q: How do I get students their grades?

A: Most course management systems provide for this. Students have a unique user name in each class for logging in to the secure system. When they enter, or log in to, the system, their user name accesses their records and provides them a place to check for grades. Grades on a paper or an exam can be sent automatically to the students' view of their own records as well. Many systems also provide additional tools to send feedback to the students.

Assessment Used to Aid Student Learning. If monitoring student learning is summative in nature for the purpose of record keeping and grading, assessment used to aid student learning might be considered more formative in nature. Timely feedback, or assessment, on what students are doing and how well they are progressing makes it possible for them to learn. Gagné's (1997) research on the internal processes of learning indicates that learning cannot occur without assessment. Dick and Carey (2001) suggest that there are three basic times when assessment occurs: pretests, to measure prerequisite skills and prior learning; posttests, to measure whether the student has mastered the skills; and embedded tests, or exercises, to aid learning and monitor students' progress. Students who know how well they are doing on embedded exercises can then make needed adjustments in a course. The answers to homework problems can help an instructor locate areas where a student appears to be struggling. If proper remediation is given, the student can improve in those areas and ultimately in the class. In this section, we focus on formative assessment provided by embedded assessments and suggest that within an on-line course, communication itself can be used as an assessment tool.

Face-to-face courses rely on communication between professors and students. In Web-based courses, communication and interaction are important tools in helping to guide student learning. The two most common ways to interact are text-based synchronous communications, or chat sessions, and text-based asynchronous communications, or bulletin boards.

Common Questions About Synchronous Communications

Q: What is chat?

A: Communicating by typing messages to another person in real time. Formal chats can be recorded, or logged, by the system and the transcripts kept. Informal chats may exist only for the duration of the chat and not be recorded. Chats can involve one-to-one interaction but more typically involve many-to-many communication. One way to think of chats is as a kind of text-based conference call. More than two people are on the line at a time discussing some point. It might also be compared to citizens band radios where anybody with access to a particular channel may participate in the discussion. In chats, as we currently understand them, the communication is done in text, with people typing their comments and submitting them to the group.

Q: What are bulletin boards?

A: Bulletin boards are electronic forums where communication is not done in real time. For instance, I might pose a question on Monday; the student might read it on Tuesday, think about it on Wednesday, and respond to the original question on Thursday. Discussions are typically threaded, which means that a common subject line groups them. If a member of the discussion responds to an original message, it is shown in a physically proximate location to the original message. Bulletin boards are used primarily for communication by class participants about particular topics. Topics for discussion on bulletin board may be reading assignments, assigned problems, or other topics submitted by the instructor or students.

Q: How do you use chats to aid learning?

A: Conceptually, in the same way you use class discussions. You or the students may pose a question, and class participants respond to it. The biggest concern for chats is the speed at which they take place. In face-to-face verbal communication, there are naturally occurring physical and social cues that let you know whether a person is still speaking or finished speaking and it is your turn to speak. In chats, these cues do not exist naturally. Because chats rely so heavily on typing skill and speed, slow typists might be interrupted before they finish their thoughts. In chats, the person with the best keyboarding skills can often dominate the discussions. In face-to-face classes, teachers can manage discussions with established rules of conduct. For instance, students may need to raise their hand to be called on in order to speak. Students can see each other or see the professor, and hold their comments until it is acceptable for them to speak.

Because so many students may be unfamiliar with chat environments, it is necessary to establish rules of conduct for the class. If fifteen or twenty students are all typing at once, chaos can reign very quickly. One way of controlling chats is to establish rules of conduct for chats. Basic rules might be to have the students type a question mark when they want to ask a question or an exclamation mark when they wish to make a comment. This text cue can mimic the social cue of raising one's hand in class to ask a question. The teacher can then call on the student to ask the question when there is an appropriate pause in the current discussion. (For more detail on chat conventions, see Harmon and Jones, forthcoming.)

Q: If I don't type fast, should I not use chats?

A: It depends on what you are comfortable with, but there is a simple trick that we have used successfully in on-line classes to assist with slow typing speeds. If you are leading a discussion on Planck's constant, as an example, and you have done this in classes many times, you know where many of the questions will arise. If there are statements that you know you want to make or can anticipate having to make, type them in advance and be prepared to copy them from an open text document and paste it into the chat software. This saves you typing time and helps you prepare for the course discussion. Also consider spelling and grammar. Because you must type so quickly, revising text or checking the spelling of a word can cause long, sometimes pedagogically inappropriate pauses in the discussion. We recommend that you not treat chats with the same editorial rigor that you would a research paper. Most people make mistakes when using text as a quick discussion tool, and those mistakes should be overlooked as long as they do not hinder the discussions.

Q: How do I use bulletin boards to aid in student learning?

A: Much in the same way that you might use class discussions. You must collect information from individuals and evaluate it in a manner that helps them master the content. The information gathered from the bulletin board can conceptually be likened to class discussions. However, instead of taking place in real time, people have time to think, reflect, and post their ideas. Bulletin boards are typically logged, or saved. You can sort student messages by each student, and analyze them to determine the degree to which an individual student is making meaningful and reflective contributions to a discussion. At a more rudimentary level, most course management systems provide counts of how many messages each student has posted and has "read." Note that the course management system is counting only whether a student has opened a message, not whether he or she has actually read it. We recommend that you use message counts only to set the standard for the most basic level of participation in a course. For example, a student who has read fewer than 50 percent of the posts on a bulletin board cannot make a grade higher than a C in a course. However, a student who has read 100 percent of the posts is not guaranteed any particular grade either. Better grades require a more qualitative assessment of participation based on individual contributions to the class.

Q: Which is better: the bulletin board or the chatroom?

A: Although the choice clearly depends on purpose, we advise caution with chats for two reasons. First, text-based chats are hard to do for longer than about ninety minutes. The speed with which they move and the mental and visual focus they take are quite draining on instructor and students. Second, students tend to equate synchronous meetings more than asynchronous meetings with class time. Chats can lull students into thinking that the chat session is the class.

The bulletin board is a tool that promotes reflection and keeps people in communication for the duration of the course. Because of the relatively more relaxed pace of the bulletin board, people have more processing time and more opportunities to say what they mean rather than just what they can type.

Chats are good places to build community, and they can be pedagogically beneficial when used judiciously. They do require quick thinking and good skills in order to be used effectively. While you build those skills, we recommend that you take advantage of the bulletin board as a place to hold discussions.

Assessment Used to Evaluate a Course. Course effectiveness is often monitored by student success. Whereas a single assessment of learning outcomes, such as a final exam, can provide an overall indication of the effectiveness of the course, more frequent assessments of learning outcomes and careful monitoring of them can pinpoint exactly where the course succeeds and where it fails. Often, exam scores and student course evaluations are used as common measures of effectiveness. Depending on the purpose of your evaluation of the course, other options are available (Branzburg, 2001).

Common Questions About Evaluating Course Effectiveness

Q: How do I evaluate my course?

A: Evaluate the course based on student learning (Did they learn the material?), student perceptions (Did they perceive the course environment as good or bad?), and course functionality (Were there significant technical problems with the class?). In our experience, existing course evaluations for universities will need to be rewritten to reflect the nature of the on-line course.

Because so much of the interaction is logged, it is possible to conduct various analyses of the communications during and after the class. Harmon and Jones (2002) demonstrate a qualitative analysis of student responses and Macklin, Harmon, Jones, and Evans (2002) a tool to automate and quantify the analysis of text-based responses. Formal analyses are possible and desirable, and less formal reflections on your classes can be invaluable. Reflection on teaching makes us better teachers. Face-to-face classes do not log discussions word for word, and we must rely on our memory to reconstruct interactions. On-line classes are different in this regard. Because the course interactions are logged, the data are available long after the class is offered and provide reflective teachers with many opportunities to look at what happened in the class. The data that the course management system collects are impressive. They can tell who logged in to the system when and how long they stayed. You can look at the days and times people logged in to get an understanding of use patterns as well. Once you establish the questions you wish to answer, the course management system will allow you to mine the data for those answers.

Q: How do I use these analyses?

A: Any data collected on a course can be used to improve subsequent offerings of it. In addition, data may be used to document the time and effort you spend in the class. It may also be possible for you to use the data from an on-line class for more traditional forms of scholarship. Given that many universities have chosen to embrace Boyer's comprehensive description of scholarship (1990), assessment used to evaluate the course can provide concrete data on many aspects of scholarship. In our experience, it is typically more time-intensive to teach on-line than to teach face-to-face, and faculty loads should reflect this. The data collected from the course can help make this case in striking detail.

Conclusion

Assessment and on-line courses intersect at two key vertices: assessment within the course and assessment of the course. Assessment in the course exists as the summative evaluation of learners and how well they have done and the formative evaluation of learners and how well they are doing so that they might make proper adjustments within the course. Assessment of the course consists of questions of both how much learning took place and how well the course environment worked for the learners. The tools of on-line courses help instructors to conduct these assessments. Bulletin boards and chats provide opportunities for both interaction within the course and evaluation of the course. Built-in technology, such as digital drop boxes, provide sophisticated tools to facilitate assessment in the course. But assessment in on-line courses is not without its problems as well. Issues as mild as typing speed and as complex as on-line plagiarism abound.

Given the advantages and disadvantages of on-line courses, we conclude that assessment in on-line courses can be at least as robust as in face-to-face courses, if not more so. Tracking and logging tools provide instructors with robust and complex data to look not only at the products of student learning, such as papers, projects, and exams, but also the learning process as documented by the on-line discussion tools and manifested in posts to the bulletin board and discussions in the chats. Given time to explore these data, professors can use on-line courses to maximize the effectiveness of any course to help students not only obtain information, but to gain clear understanding of what they know and why they know it.

References

Boyer, E. L. *Scholarship Reconsidered: Priorities of the Professorate.* San Francisco: Jossey-Bass, 1997 (originally published 1990).

Branzburg, J. "How Well Is It Working? Customizing Your Technology Assessment." *Technology and Learning,* 2001 (21)7, 24.

Dick, W., and Carey, L. *The Systematic Design of Instruction.* (5th ed.) Glenview, Ill.: Scott, Foresman, 2001.

Gagné, R. *The Conditions of Learning and Theory of Instruction.* New York: Holt, Rinehart and Winston, 1997.

Harmon, S. W., and Jones, M. G. "The Five Levels of Web Use in Education: Factors to Consider in Planning On-Line Courses." *Educational Technology,* 1999, 39(6), 28–32.

Harmon, S. W., and Jones, M. G. "An Analysis of Situated Web-Based Instruction." *Educational Media International,* Dec. 2001, 38(4), 271–280.

Jones, M. G., and Harmon, S. W. "Using Internet Based Learning in Higher Education: A Systemic Model." In *Proceedings of the 2001 International Conference of the Association of Educational Communications and Technology.* Bloomington, Ind.: Association of Educational Communications and Technology, 2002.

Jones, M. G., Harmon, S. W., and Lowther, D. "Integrating Web-Based Learning in an Educational System: A Framework for Implementation." In R. A. Reiser and J. V. Dempsey (eds.), *Trends and Issues in Instructional Design and Technology.* Upper Saddle River, N.J.: Merrill/Prentice Hall, 2002.

Macklin, T., Harmon, S. W., Jones, M. G., and Evans, W. "Cognitive Engagement in Web-Based Learning: A Content Analysis of Students' On-Line Discussions." In *Proceedings of the 2001 International Conference of the Association of Educational Communications and Technology.* Bloomington, Ind.: Association of Educational Communications and Technology, 2002.

Niguidula, D. "Picturing Performance with Digital Portfolios." *Educational Leadership,* 1997, 55(3), 26–30.

President's Committee of Advisors on Science and Technology. *Report to the President on the Use of Technology to Strengthen K-12 Education in the United States.* [http//:www.ostp.gov/PCAST/k-12ed.html]. 1997.

Seels, B., and Richey, R. C. *Instructional Technology: The Definition and Domains of the Field.* Washington, D.C.: Association for Educational Communications and Technology, 1994.

MARSHALL G. JONES is an assistant professor of instructional design and technology in the Richard W. Riley College of Education at Winthrop University, Rock Hill, South Carolina.

STEPHEN W. HARMON is the director of educational technology for the College of Education and an associate professor of instructional technology at Georgia State University, Atlanta.

3

Professors can establish rubrics for assessing participation in chatroom discussions and the content of student contributions in both chatrooms and bulletin boards.

Assessing Student Work from Chatrooms and Bulletin Boards

John F. Bauer

> The key to success in a distance-learning classroom is not which technologies are used but how they are used and what information is communicated using the technologies.
> —Simonson (2000, p. 29)

With advances in Web-based technology, the on-line class has become a common option in higher education. Even professors who are not tech-savvy are using course management systems to click into the world of digital learning.

Launching the virtual class may be the easy part. An emergent problem is that assessing student work in the on-line learning medium poses new twists in traditional assessment methodology (see Chapter Two). This is particularly true when the professor is confronted with assessing student work that is posted in two common on-line forums: the chatroom and the bulletin board. Traditional notions of collecting and grading papers have little currency in these two fast-paced print mediums, where student work is often submitted daily.

Professors can take some comfort in the fact that a numerical grading guideline (that is, a rubric) has the potential to work just as well for the chatroom and bulletin board of the on-line class as it does in the four-walled classroom. If using a rubric makes sense to professors, three options are available for creating grading criteria: they can write their own, seek advice and consent from their students, as some have suggested (Anderson, 1998), or use a rubric with preestablished guidelines as found in the literature. This chapter offers a broad view of why chatrooms and bulletin boards are popular with professors and suggests the use of rubrics for making logical and

NEW DIRECTIONS FOR TEACHING AND LEARNING, no. 91, Fall 2002 © Wiley Periodicals, Inc.

Exhibit 3.1. Terms Associated with Chatrooms and Bulletin Boards

---

- *Asynchronous.* Delayed talk on-line. Bulletin board.
- *BBS.* Bulletin board system. The technical connectivity between computer modems that makes the bulletin board possible.
- *Blackboard.* Common course management system for on-line courses.
- *Chatiquette.* The informal code of behavior, or etiquette, for participation in chat. Do's and don'ts.
- *CMC.* Computer-mediated communication. Refers to systems and networks that computers use to transfer, store, and retrieve information, that is, normal, interactive Web sites in use for on-line courses (Clay-Warner and Marsh, 2000).
- *Computer conferencing.* Generic term associated with bulletin boards. Can cause some confusion since conferencing is also possible synchronically in a chatroom medium.
- *Discussion forum.* Generic term associated with bulletin boards.
- *High-touch class.* A class with regular face-to-face meetings.
- *Hosting and posting.* Casual reference to chatrooms and bulletin boards.
- *Interactive Web site.* A site that allows viewers to type communications to the Web site. On-line courses use interactive sites.
- *Low-touch class.* A class that meets almost entirely on-line.
- *Newsgroup.* A bulletin board.
- *Real time.* Live, synchronous communication; chat.
- *Synchronous.* Live talk on-line; chat.
- *WBI.* Web-based instruction. The progenitor of the on-line class. From a technical standpoint, the WBI and on-line class are synonymous. However, evolution has suggested that WBI connotes on-line education more global in nature, attaching greater significance to World Wide Web networking and often connecting schools with those in other states and countries in order to build knowledge from a "networked society" (Romiszowski, 1999, p. 340). Moreover, with a focus on regional or international communication, WBI is more likely to stress cultural sensitivity (Reeves and Reeves, 1999).
- *WebCT.* Common course management system for professors to use to launch interactive class Web sites for on-line instruction.

---

just assessments of student postings in the chatroom and bulletin board. (Exhibit 3.1 provides a selected list of the technical and casual jargon associated with chatrooms and bulletin boards.)

The Chatroom and Assessment

The technology for the professor's Web site is derived from commercial Internet sites that have had patrons chatting away on various topics for years. In the academic arena, the chatroom allows the entire class, or simply two or more members, to meet on-line at the same time and have a lively text-generated conversation. In this sense, it is the on-line environment that comes closest to simulating a regular class meeting. The chatroom allows for brainstorming sessions, discussions of hot topics, team planning, and question-and-answer forums (McCampbell, 2000). Berzsenyi (2000) notes also that chatrooms allow professors to engage the greatest number

Exhibit 3.2. Rubric for Assessing Chat Participation

Number of Points	Skills
9–10	Logs into chat in a timely manner; fully participates during entire period on a consistent basis; follows discussion thread; responds readily to direct questions. All responses are self-initiated.
7–8	Logs into chat in a timely manner; generally keeps up with discussion thread but will participate in some topics more than others; may need an occasional prompt from the chat manager.
5–6	Is sometimes late to log in. Spotty participation; may disappear from chat for long periods of time; contributes infrequently; often requires prompting.
1–4	May miss chat altogether without explanation; displays little evidence of following discussion; rarely participates freely.

of students in discussion at the same time, involve students in collaborative work, and get them engaged in writing for real audiences. Moreover, students are able to share in the teaching as well as the learning in the chat environment.

Grading class participation can have a positive effect on the ability of students to demonstrate growth in critical thinking, active learning, and their ability to develop skills in active discourse (Bean and Peterson, 1998). It follows that the professor who values student participation in face-to-face classroom discussions to the extent that such participation is scored by a grade will also want a measurement strategy for chatroom discussions. Exhibit 3.2 provides a suggested numerical grading guideline (rubric) for assessing participation in the chatroom. In an on-line class, professors who place little or no value on participation in chat run the risk of talking to themselves. Students in a regular class can often be nudged into contributing to a discussion, but there is no prodding a student who has not logged into the chatroom. An additional feature of the chatroom that makes reviewing student participation possible is that sessions are automatically saved, or archived, for easy review.

Slow typists are at a disadvantage when participation is assessed. Typing ability and speed have a great influence on chat participation, and the more accurately a person can type influences the perceived credibility of the contribution (Harmon and Jones, 1999).

Many professors may be satisfied with the general nature of assessing simple participation in chat. Others might want to emphasize to students that logging into the chatroom and participating in the conversation is an important step, but a consistent quality of contributions is the substance of a valuable discussion. These professors may have had the experience of witnessing a chatroom that becomes an unfocused free-for-all, somewhat like a class before the professor walks in.

Exhibit 3.3. Rubric for Assessing the Content of Chat Contributions

Number of Points	Skills
9–10	Comments adhere to chat conventions, follow discussion threads, are coherent. Contributions demonstrate a grasp of key concepts; there are frequent questions and a willingness to challenge the thinking of others.
7–8	Comments adhere to chat conventions, follow discussion threads, are mostly easy to understand. Contributions are usually relevant, and there are occasional questions.
5–6	Occasional lapses from chat conventions. Comments are often short, may lack relevance and seem forced; some incoherent remarks go nowhere.
1–4	Responses at this level contribute almost nothing to chat. Attempts at lengthy responses are largely unintelligible.

Note: Chat conventions refers to an informal code of behavior governing what should and should not be said in the chatroom.

To preempt an unruly chat, consider posting a rubric that looks something like the one shown in Exhibit 3.3. Note that precise language and typing skills are not listed as premiums to high scoring unless they interfere with coherence.

The Bulletin Board and Assessment

Every course Web site contains a *forum,* a place where class members can post messages. Controlled by the professor, the forum provides topics and comments that call for student responses. Once the professor has opened a forum and provided a thread for discussion, the students can type their contributions into a special response window located on a separate Web page. When the comments are written the way they are intended, the student clicks the Submit button, automatically sending the contribution to the forum site for viewing by the whole class. The student either responds to a comment already posted or starts a new discussion thread by clicking the appropriate button.

The asynchronous nature of the bulletin board makes it a popular tool for on-line professors. Compared to the chatroom, it is much easier to facilitate and is not dependent on the clock. The professor can open the bulletin board for business at the beginning of class and leave it open until the end.

Although bulletin boards lack the immediacy of live communication, they allow a more directed and lasting flow of concepts, ideas, and opinions (McCampbell, 2000). Bolstered by research and the resulting use of direct quotations and citations, students can make impressive cases for their points of view. They can take their time to reflect, craft contributions thoughtfully, and pay strict attention to usage, grammar, and spelling. Nonnative speakers may feel more confident about posting on the bulletin board because they have more time to process their thoughts before submitting them (Khan, 1999).

Bulletin boards have other positive features:

- The bulletin board makes possible a reflective follow-up to chatroom topics.
- Postings allow for the use of attachments. Students working on group projects can complete their work on a separate word-processed file and send it along to the forum.
- Students can write on their own time. Without the pressure of a class to attend, they can work at meeting a posting deadline when it best suits them.
- Professors can check the bulletin boards as often or as infrequently as desired. As long as the Web site is open, there is a permanent record of postings. This is beneficial to both students and professor.

The assessment of student work on the bulletin board differs significantly from that in the chatroom. If the analogue to chat is the classroom discussion, the analogue to the bulletin board is the hard-copy essay. In this sense, postings can be set to the same criteria that the professor establishes for grading the essay.

Unlike the quick-thinking and quick-typing milieu of chat, all students have the time to produce their best work before submitting it for view on the bulletin board. Exhibit 3.4 suggests a rubric for assessing the content of student postings to the bulletin board.

Exhibit 3.4. Rubric for Assessing Student Postings on the Bulletin Board

Number of Points	Skills
9–10	Demonstrates excellence in grasping key concepts; critiques work of others; stimulates discussion; provides ample citations for support of opinions; readily offers new interpretations of discussion material. Ideas are expressed clearly, concisely; uses appropriate vocabulary.
7–8	Shows evidence of understanding most major concepts; will offer an occasional divergent viewpoint or challenge; shows some skill in support for opinions. Some signs of disorganization with expression; transition wording may be faulty.
5–6	Has mostly shallow grasp of the material; rarely takes a stand on issues; offers inadequate levels of support. Poor language use garbles much of the message; only an occasional idea surfaces clearly; expression seems disjointed; overuse of the simple sentence and a redundancy with words and commentary; paragraphs often appear unrelated to each other. This student requires constant prompting for contributions.
1–4	A minimal posting of material. Shows no significant understanding of material. Language is mostly incoherent. Does not respond readily to prompting.

Source: Adapted from Bauer and Anderson (2000).

Conclusion

As professors move in the direction of providing some course work on-line, they may be interested in using rubrics to assess students' writing in chatrooms or for bulletin boards. Indeed, the primary means of communication between class members and professors in on-line courses are chatrooms and bulletin boards. This chapter offers a guide for professors seeking means to assess student contributions in these two important environments using rubrics that measure degrees of participation and content, or quality, of work submitted.

References

Anderson, R. S. "Why Talk About Different Ways to Grade? The Shift from Traditional Assessment to Alternative Assessment." In R. S. Anderson and B. W. Speck (eds.), *Changing the Way We Grade Student Performance: Classroom Assessment and the New Learning Paradigm.* New Directions in Teaching and Learning, no. 74. San Francisco: Jossey-Bass, 1998.

Bauer, J. F., and Anderson, R. S. "Evaluating Students' Written Performance in the On-Line Class." In R. E. Weiss, D. S. Knowlton, and B. W. Speck (eds.), *Principles of Effective Learning in the On-Line Class.* New Directions in Teaching and Learning, no. 84. San Francisco: Jossey-Bass, 2000.

Bean, J. C., and Peterson, D. "Grading Classroom Participation." In R. S. Anderson and B. W. Speck (eds.), *Changing the Way We Grade Student Performance: Classroom Assessment and the New Learning Paradigm.* New Directions in Teaching and Learning, no. 74. San Francisco: Jossey-Bass, 1998.

Berzsenyi, C. A. "How to Conduct a Course-Based Computer Chat Room: Enabling a Space for Active Learning." *Teaching English in the Two-Year College,* 2000, *28*(2), 165–174.

Clay-Warner, J., and Marsh, K. "Implementing Computer Mediated Communication in the College Classroom." *Journal of Educational Computing Research,* 2000, *23*(3), 257–274.

Harmon, S. W., and Jones, M. G. "The Five Levels of Web Use in Education: Factors to Consider in Planning On-Line Courses." *Educational Technology,* 1999, *39*(6), 28–32.

Khan, B. H. "Web-Based Instruction: What Is It and Why Is It?" In B. H. Khan (ed.), *Web-Based Instruction.* Englewood Cliffs, N.J.: Educational Technology Publications, 1999.

McCampbell, B. "Toys or Tools? On-Line Bulletin Boards and Chat Rooms." *Principal Leadership* (High School Ed.), 2000, *1*(3), 73–74.

Reeves, T. C., and Reeves, P. M. "Effective Dimensions of Interactive Learning on the World Wide Web." In B. H. Khan (ed.), *Web-Based Instruction.* Englewood Cliffs, N.J.: Educational Technology Publications, 1999.

Romiszowski, A. J. "Web-Based Distance Learning and Teaching: Revolutionary Invention or Reaction to Necessity?" In B. H. Khan (ed.), *Web-Based Instruction.* Englewood Cliffs, N.J.: Educational Technology Publications, 1999.

Simonson, M. "Making Decisions: The Use of Electronic Technology in On-Line Classrooms." In R. E. Weiss, D. S. Knowlton, and B. W. Speck (eds.), *Principles of Effective Learning in the On-Line Class.* New Directions in Teaching and Learning, no. 84. San Francisco: Jossey-Bass, 2000.

JOHN F. BAUER *is an assistant professor in the department of instructional technology at Towson University, Maryland.*

4

This chapter discusses procedures that on-line instructors uses when "marking the screen" or using separate attachments for commentary. It explores the use of e-mail as the analogue of face-to-face conferencing for providing feedback.

Assessing Students' Written Projects

Robert Gray

Students in on-line courses exist only in how they represent themselves through their writing. As Condon (2000, p. 50) points out, traditional classrooms exist apart from the class members, but in the virtual classroom, "if there is no writing, there is no classroom. The participants are what they write." This presents an interesting assessment challenge for on-line instructors, especially those in disciplines that normally are not writing intensive. Most of the literature on writing in on-line classrooms is not very helpful, since it deals with composition classrooms, usually networked computer labs in which students synchronously share the same physical space. Furthermore, most of the current research on on-line assessment deals with the instructional theory behind such assessment rather than ways to do the assessment. This chapter focuses on methods of providing feedback to students in regard to the assessment of their writing.

Formal Versus Informal Writing

Unless you are teaching a composition course, you want to ensure that informal types of writing can indeed be informal because the formulation and communication of ideas are more important in most courses than typing and proofreading skills. From the perspectives of both the instructor and students, journal entries, threaded discussions, and chats should be focused on ideas, not grammar. Because of this, try not to concern yourself with sentence-level issues in students' writing; rather, let the students' writing make their "thought visible" (Smith, 1998, p. 1). This is not to say that you should not expect good writing. You can and should tell students that you do expect it; you should even insist that they proofread and edit carefully, but also let them

Exhibit 4.1. Rubric for Assessing Participation in Group Projects

Activity	Percentage of Final Grade
Participation in group threaded discussion	10 percent
Participation in group chats	10 percent
Group project grade	40 percent
Participation in drafting process	20 percent
Participation in peer review of drafts	20 percent

know that the communication of good thinking is the primary basis for their grade on such assignments.

Formal assignments and projects can be more demanding of students' writing skills. Indeed, as a rule of thumb, you should weigh writing skills in an on-line course just as you would in the traditional classroom, and the nature of the project should determine the degree of polish necessary.

Participation. The types of projects that can be assigned in an on-line class are virtually endless. You can creatively duplicate all kinds of classroom presentations on-line. In fact, it is easier in many ways to manage and assess group collaboration in on-line student projects because of the tools available for course platform systems (examples are eCollege, WebCT, and Blackboard). These systems provide group chatrooms, threaded discussion boards, and document-sharing areas that allow you to monitor participation much more effectively than you can on campus. Exhibit 4.1 provides an example of a rubric for assessing participation.

Students can produce slide shows, research papers, and multimedia projects for presentations and can give "oral" presentations in the chatroom. Certain cameras even make it possible for students to give live presentations on-line. For the time being, however, written projects are the easiest and likely the most used format.

Designing Assignments. When assigning written projects, it is wise to require more than just the final product. Requiring multiple stages of the writing process protects against academic dishonesty and incorporates other kinds of activities into the assignment, such as research, student interaction, peer review, drafting, and revision. You should also design assignments to minimize the likelihood of paper shopping. Despite all of the wonderful and powerful Internet tools and resources available to improve student learning and achievement, perhaps the most used are the buy-a-paper sites like SchoolSucks (http://schoolsucks.com/termpapers.html) and Evil House of Cheat (http://www.cheathouse.com).

The use of on-line peer review workshops is an excellent way to protect against cheating. More important, it is an easy-to-design collaborative activity that strengthens critical thinking skills and leads to better writing. Furthermore, peer review transfers some of the assessment responsibility from the instructor to the class members, which gives them a greater degree of ownership of the course. This sense of ownership will lead to a higher level of engagement and, ultimately, better student outcomes.

The most basic method to set up an on-line peer review is to have students e-mail each other their drafts, but the group tools, document-sharing areas, and threaded discussion tools in your course platform system, which allow you to stay in the loop, can also be used. You will need to give students explicit directions on what to do, from the logistics of how to exchange papers to the mechanics of providing feedback.

When you design a written project for on-line students, your methods and theories of assessment will play a part in that design, and it is important to make sure that the assignment and assessment are instructionally relevant by focusing on priority learning outcomes (Isaacson, 1999). Another important issue in assessing these kinds of projects is how you will grade them.

Marking the Screen

A vast amount of research has been done on the use of artificial intelligence to grade essays (see http://www.knowledge-technologies.com), but until (and if) we reach the point where that is both academically acceptable and financially accessible, papers will still have to be graded the old-fashioned way, by the professor. Providing feedback on a computer screen is known as *marking the screen.*

Submission Guidelines. Traditional classrooms work on a set of unstated assumptions that are not valid in the virtual classroom. You cannot stand at the front of the classroom and tell the students to hand in their papers. An on-line classroom mandates detailed instructions.

First, decide how students are to submit their papers:

- By e-mail as an attached file
- Through a feature of the course platform, such as a document-sharing area or a student drop box
- By mail or fax

In most cases, substantial written assignments are best submitted electronically as word processor files. It is much easier for students to compose and edit on their own word processor than inside an on-line course (for instance, in an on-line journal or threaded discussion). It is also easier for you to read and edit their work with your word processor. Also, if students use word processors, they have the benefit of spell-check, and, perhaps more important, they will always have a copy of the file on disk.

File Type Guidelines. Assignments must be in a file type that your computer can read. Traditionally (if there is such a thing in on-line learning), the standard methodology has been to have students save documents as Rich Text Format (.rtf) files. Most recent word processors also have a

Save As feature to save files as other programs' file types, and virtually any computer capable of handling an on-line course will have a word processor that can save as Microsoft Word 97 or WordPerfect 5x. Newer versions of Word and WordPerfect are forward and backward compatible with those versions, so you can safely require students to save their files as whatever kind of major word processor you choose. This compatibility is important because working with files that you are used to handling and that your word processor automatically recognizes saves you time and effort.

It is a good idea to have students send you an attached file early in the course to make sure that you can open and read their documents. This will save some worry for both of you when the major projects are due. It is also important to give students clear guidelines on how to title files and e-mails that they submit. An in-box full of files labeled Paper2.doc will only cause you confusion.

Features for Providing Feedback. Once you receive students' papers, you need to provide feedback. Many on-line instructors print out electronically submitted papers and mark them in the traditional way. However, with the inserting comments and tracking changes features of modern word processors like Word and WordPerfect, you can "mark the screen" even more effectively than you could with the traditional red pen. These features are useful for marking final papers and also in the writing process, both for your purposes and for student peer review. They are compatible when converting a file from Word to WordPerfect and vice versa.

Inserting Comments. An "insert-comment" feature allows you to comment without disrupting the flow of the student's writing. When you add a comment, the portion of the text that you are commenting on turns yellow, and when the student hovers the mouse pointer over the yellow area, the comment will appear in a pop-up box. If it is a rough draft that you are reviewing, the student can view your comment, make the appropriate changes, and then delete the comment without the original text being affected by your marks. Other advantages of this feature are that comments are not limited to the space available in the margin, and legibility is not an issue for students of handwriting-challenged instructors.

To insert comments, consult the help manual with your word processing program for specific details. You can also insert pen and voice comments if your computer is equipped with a pen mechanism or microphone, respectively. This can help to bring the human element into the on-line workshop environment. One drawback of voice comments is that they result in huge file sizes, so returning the document to the student could cause downloading issues.

Tracking Changes. Inserting comments is most useful for remarking on or questioning a student's content, ideas, or organization. For mechanical and stylistic corrections or other editing changes at the sentence level, tracking changes is another excellent feature available in Word and WordPerfect. This feature allows you to make clear and legible corrections to a student's writing while preserving the original. When you make a change, the feature changes the color of and draws a line through the original text; it shows the changes or corrections in the new color. The feature also puts a vertical line in the left margin denoting where a change has been made. The student can then accept or reject each change by right-clicking on the edited text.

What to Mark. Typically, on-line students feel more alienated from their instructor than traditional students do, so be careful to shape feedback accordingly. Emphasize the positive while clearly explaining the negative, and always remind students that you are willing to explain and discuss your position further.

To allow time for such substantial feedback, consider adopting a short-hand system for marking common mistakes. An excellent example is Smith's "A Quick Guide to Lite Marking" (1998). Another suggestion is to use two highlighting colors, with one color for strengths and the other for errors. In Word 98 and 2000, highlight the text, and click the Highlight button on the Formatting or Reviewing toolbar. In any case, do not spend too much time or effort at the sentence level. Insert marginal comments and mechanical corrections only when absolutely necessary, and do not "scatter buckshot all over the paper"; this will only overwhelm the student and reduce the effectiveness of your commentary (Wollaeger, 2001). If you do want to focus on the mechanics of students' writing, rather than typing lengthy explanations, provide hypertext references to on-line resources that provide explanations for their particular problems. You can do this by creating a master list of sites and then pasting the URL or hyperlink into their paper.

On-Line Conferencing

The assessment of written projects should not end with electronic marking You can easily use e-mail as an analogue of face-to-face conferencing. This might require some effort (and patience) initially to help students who are uncomfortable with the technology (Anderson-Inman, 1997), but it can be an effective medium for tutorials.

The first step is providing ample and relevant comments on-screen. You should also encourage students to ask follow-up questions about their papers, and then answer them in a timely and substantive manner. You can take advantage of the nature of e-mail to lead students to make discoveries about their writing by requiring them to tackle their writing problems in writing (Jackson, 2000).

You can use a chatroom for synchronous conferencing if immediate feedback is necessary or desirable. This can be done on a regular "office hours" basis or by appointment. Private discussions of this kind should take place in a chat environment that is not archived. And although we tend to get caught up in available technologies, we should remember that a telephone conversation can be effective as well.

Conclusion

Regardless of your discipline or pedagogical approach, written projects should play a significant role in all on-line courses if assessment is to be effective and have integrity. Marking papers on-screen and handling e-mail might take some getting used to, but you will quickly adjust and develop a system. You will probably change the Zoom setting of your word processor to make the print size larger, and you might even learn how to set up your e-mail program to use groups and rules to sort students' papers into their own folder, but in any case, you will find that you can handle written projects quite effectively in the on-line environment. You might even start having your on-campus students submit their projects electronically.

References

Anderson-Inman, L. "OWLs: Online Writing Labs." *Journal of Adolescent and Adult Literacy*, 1997, *40,* 650–654.

Condon, W. "Virtual Space, Real Participation: Dimensions and Dynamics of a Virtual Classroom." In S. Harrington, R. Rickly, and M. Day (eds.), *The On-Line Writing Classroom.* Cresskill, N.J.: Hampton, 2000.

Isaacson, S. "Instructionally Relevant Writing Assessment." *Reading and Writing Quarterly,* 1999 *15,* 29–49.

Jackson, J. A. "Interfacing the Faceless: Maximizing the Advantages of On-Line Tutoring." *Writing Lab Newsletter,* 2000, 25(2).

Smith, R. "A Quick Guide to Lite Marking." [http://www.indiana.edu/~wts/cwp/quick-guide.html]. 1998. Access date: July 27, 2001.

Wollaeger, M. "Notes on Grading Papers." [http://www.vanderbilt.edu/cwp/grading.htm]. Access date: July 27, 2001.

ROBERT GRAY is an academic services consultant for eCollege and a doctoral student in instructional technology at the University of Alabama, Tuscaloosa.

5

Assessing the student group poses rewards and challenges for on-line instructors. This chapter offers five principles for assessment, derived from field research among on-line instructors, with some cautionary discussion on how to handle plagiarism.

Group Assessment in the On-Line Learning Environment

John A. Nicolay

Academic assessment engenders opportunities for students to grow as intelligent agents of their disciplines. Within the learning community, we gauge success through formal and informal feedback to the participants. This is no less true of the group experience. Students routinely engage in collaborative scholarship in their classes through group projects, generally team efforts to produce a single essay on a topic in support of class learning objectives. The group project is a popular way for on-line educators to mimic social exchanges similar to those that might emerge in traditional classroom environments when individuals are compelled to work together to achieve a common outcome. The hope is that the ability to navigate differences and forge alliances will reside with students beyond the constraints of the course itself. However, the on-line experience can be so negative that students willfully shun the experience if given the election opportunity. Teamwork is not for everyone, yet we make it so as educators in electing this form of exercise. Educators find themselves compelled to make sense of the experience, rationalize its appropriateness, and invariably wrestle with the dynamics of the interaction between people who depend on each other to meet personal goals.

The group exercise takes on a variety of forms, and generally assessment of this performance settles into the "all for one and one for all" flavor,

The survey reported in this study was an open-ended instrument with follow-up discussions. I extend my appreciation to Alan Carswell and Cam McEachern for their assistance in this regard.

although some instructors require students to self-assess or to assess their peers (for a critical review, see Reynolds and Trehan, 2000). Unless the group is disbanded or the faculty member requires that students take ownership in their specific contributions to the project, the group is assessed as a unit and the grade distributed evenly regardless of how individual members might have contributed to the final submission or how they judge their peers' worthiness in the group effort. This can be problematic (Weisband and Atwater, 1999).

Invariably, some form of faculty assessment always takes place for group exercises, although this assessment may not always be understood by the students or rigorously applied by the assessor. Other chapters in this volume adequately defend the principles of assessment in academic environments. This chapter proposes five broad assessment guidelines that evolved through survey research done at two major universities with extensive experience in on-line education.

Faculty at Troy State University and the University of Maryland University College provided feedback on their general practices regarding student assessment with a narrow inquiry into their practices toward group experiences. They report that the group assessment experience cannot be disassociated from the overall class performance requirements. Faculty begin their courses by discussing the overall evaluation experience. Four basic components of formal on-line assessment emerged: (1) term projects produced by the individual student, (2) periodic participation within the course through electronic conversations or individually submitted reports, (3) examinations, and (4) the group experience. In each case, the professor begins the course with a detailed report on term expectations and how these expectations are to be met. This report is followed by a question-and-answer dialogue on the term requirements.

The Learning and Teaching Context

Both Troy State University and the University of Maryland University College use a Web interface engine that allows for individual postings in a discussion forum format for all class members and a restricted forum to which only assigned members of the class have access and is used for group discussions. Group discussions can take place in chatrooms, posting forums, or collaborative documents. In collaborative documents, members can add to, edit, or delete a common document. Troy State uses the Blackboard software. Maryland uses its own software engine, called Web Tycho. Neither software approach is necessary for a meaningful learning experience on-line, although these forums are a convenient archive of information transactions.

The University of Maryland provides instructors and students with narrative statements for grade performance expectations. In this way, it is clear to the students that the highest grades are reserved for the outstanding performers and the standard expectation for a graduate student is a B. Hence, the initial expectation for students and instructor is that a B will be achieved. While this alone may suffice to set a benchmark of expectations, it assists neither evaluator nor student in understanding the subjective experience of evaluation within a specific course, nor does it lend objectivity to the process. Still, institutional norms for grading are critical to the grading experience. The institution sets the tone for expectations, albeit painting only with a broad brush what these expectations are.

The Assessment Context

Instructors set the course tone at the start with concise statements of performance expectations. Students demand precision in these standards if only to judge their ranking relative to peers and dispel arising cognitive dissonance when the external standards do not match internal ones. Beyond providing students with a proportional grading scale and a clear rationale for what this scale means, faculty should frame the grading experience from their own perspective, with deference to institutional concerns (Haertel, 1999).

Ideally, grading should possess both construct validity and intergrader reliability. Investigations of the reliability and vaility of grading or assessment practices are rarely done. Most studies of assessment across the curriculum tend to deal either with grade inflation, which is the tendency to award students beyond their capability relative to other students (Lawler, 2001; Compton and Metheny, 2000), or student perceptions of grading fairness through exit surveys. The latter are notoriously flawed (Marsh and Roche, 2000; Kerridge and Mathews, 1998). Institutionally across the curriculum, grading standards would be difficult to judge, and as a consequence most universities settle on reminding faculty that the proportion of A's to B's is not satisfactory, hence forcing the introspective evaluator to rethink distribution scales rather than performance differences.

Many universities provide statements of expectations for grading outcomes. The following generic descriptions guide faculty toward crafting meaningful assessment standards:

> To achieve an A, the student or group demonstrates a mastery of learning objectives or project objectives; provides evidence of good research skills; demonstrates creative and critical thinking; and adheres to academic standards of writing style and citation. The writing arises from reasoned articulation that is both clear and persuasive.
>
> To achieve a B, which is the expectation, the student or group demonstrates mastery of learning or project objectives, reasonable research skills, a thought process through which the student has made conceptual connections between course resources and writing challenges; and adheres to the

published standards of writing style and citation. Good writing is valued of a student, and must be mastered.

The grade of C or less demonstrates that the instructor has serious concerns about the integrity of the work or the ability of the student or group to work at a graduate level.

Clearly, faculty cannot avoid subjectivity. If a B is the expectation, perhaps wisdom dictates error on the side of the B grade, not the A grade or C grade. The A grade clearly reflects excellence that is consistent across the various measurements in a class. Of all grades, instructors should be satisfied that any evaluator reviewing the C grade performer would have come to the same conclusion. Ultimately, it is the judgment of the instructor that must withstand scrutiny. It will stand as long as the instructor divorces himself or herself from capricious or arbitrary grading standards in the absence of objective testing instruments.

The Normative Aspect

The collaborative experience is foremost a social and cultural one. Like any other academic benchmark, group assessment is a critical part of the learning experience and requires standards and experience (Race, 1998). Accepting this, collaborative experiences differ from private contributions to the class. The exercises driving this experience require discursive communication skills, a surrender to the norming of the group regarding deadlines and self-evaluation, and a clear road map to closure on the exercise. Prahalad and Ramaswamy (2001) refer to this type of collaboration as the co-creation of value for which the positive affect arises along a continuum from "arm's length relationships" to "shared goals and resource leverage." The latter requires "unified information access, collaboration tools, and capacity for rapid knowledge creation and insight building" (p. 38).

The norming process reflects on how groups themselves create internal expectations for performance and then acquiesce to these standards over the term of the course. In the worst-case scenario, these norming experiences approximate what Irving Janis (1972) dubbed "groupthink." Groupthink is the process by which members of a group capitulate to the values of the strongest members while camouflaging their own points of view for the sake of comity or expediency. The instructor cannot intend this social experience, but it plays a dramatic role on how the group performs.

Five Principles of Assessment

An open-ended survey on grading practices was sent to colleagues at two universities. The twenty-two on-line educators responding identified the salient issues of constructing effective group assessment. Their responses cluster around five broadly classified principles.

Principle One: Thoroughly Structure the Project

• *Project assignment.* This is a narrative statement regarding the scope of the project and what the research and writing will involve: length, library research, citations, and format (for instance, the American Psychological Association's guidelines). Case studies represent a major class of research topics favored by many in this study. Some faculty allow students to determine their own topics following faculty approval. Others prepare a list of topics from which students select one of interest.

• *Assignment of members.* Most respondents allow students to self-select. My preference is to assign a senior class member as the group facilitator and randomly assign members from the class to complete the group composition. The typical group size is five. Random selection diffuses talent and gender, providing weaker students with opportunities to engage with stronger members. The pretense of stronger students propels weaker students who self-select topics. If assessment is to be meaningful, weaker students need opportunities to grow.

• *Suspense dates.* Suspense dates are required to keep the group moving. Consequently, respondents provide deadlines for defining individual assignments within the group, reporting first drafts, responding to comments on the first draft, responding to the final draft, and submitting to the faculty member. Group facilitators monitor suspense dates. As warranted, failure to meet suspense dates evokes a note from the faculty member to individual offenders. This contributes to an assessment criterion and could have an effect on the final grade, although I do not value it highly.

• *Writing expectations.* Teaching graduate students how to write can be daunting. Perhaps it reflects instructors' own lapses in quality or the mechanisms available to incorporate writing assessments into on-line course structure. Faculty enforce group assessment standards through the weekly writing exercises. At both Troy State and Maryland, students post weekly discussions to a conference. It is to this individual conference that other students and the instructor can provide circular narration or feedback.

For example, when I require students to participate in individual weekly conferences, I prepare a compilation of comments about their writing that I have edited in Microsoft Front Page. Off-line editing allows me to manipulate the student's text directly to point out writing and content issues that typically cannot be addressed in a posting forum directly as would traditional marginal notes on a hard-copy term paper. Front Page easily allows the editor to insert text in a different font color to differentiate it from the main body of writing. Students learn from their own efforts, the efforts of their peers, and the faculty member as expert. Failing to provide concise feedback on writing perpetuates the problems associated with weak writing. Of course, the faculty member must be competent as an editor.

Most faculty value extemporaneous contributions in weekly conference forums, but they are difficult to assess in a meaningful way. Faculty who require a weekly posting of substance find assessment easier. Hence, the student who performs at the A level as articulated will strive to do so consistently, but the faculty expectation is a B, and the student must muster to the A at each evaluation intervention. Faculty members expect students to use course resources to construct their answers, move the conversation forward from previous postings, and rely at least in part on additional resources in the answer. This provides ample opportunity to provide individually tailored critiques of each student's work.

A serious writing problem is nonattributed paraphrasing or plagiarism (McCarroll, 2001; Laird, 2001). Most professors in this study do not tolerate plagiarism or nonattributed writing yet respond casually when it is detected in the group exercise. Not all educators can detect or care to detect these problems, although there are Web sites that provide some assistance to this end. Many approach it lightly; others impose the severest sanctions: a course grade of F or, at the extreme, expulsion from the program. In our courses, professors clearly promulgate the university's position on plagiarism. Initial reactions to such activity in routine student submissions should minimally result in a reprimand with the sanction of a C grade. This leads to the anticipation that the student will clearly understand the ramifications if this behavior continues. In an electronic age, there is no more serious problem to academic writing integrity.

Principle Two: Construct the Groups and Match Membership

• *Group size matters* (Fay, Garrod, and Carletta, 2000). Five is a convenient group size, with one member of the group designated as the facilitator. This person's role is to initiate correspondence with members, start the discussion on the project scope, invite postings on dividing the workload, and make these assignments once members develop an outline of the project. The facilitator edits the project, verifies resources, and writes the introduction and the conclusion.

The survey respondents begin each class with the electronic posting of introductions. They ask each student to identify his or her status in the program of study. Selecting a senior class member is one way to identify a facilitator for the group project. The role of facilitator is critical to a successful group endeavor. The facilitator is the watchdog and project editor. My routine correspondence with group members is through its facilitator.

• *Wait two weeks to make group assignments.* This allows for late arrivals or class members who drop the course.

• *Distribute class members randomly across groups.* Student dispersal allows for a gender balance and talent distribution within the group. Other demographics may also serve as important determinants of membership, such as age, race, and ethnicity, but in a distance-learning environment, this is hard to know or to plan. Narrowing the selection demographics could also serve as a fertile ground for a later *prima facie* "arbitrary and capricious" complaint. That is, students could complain that the professor did not give careful consideration when groups were selected but formed groups using an arbitrary and capricious method.

Principle Three: Monitor and Communicate Effectively

• *Monitor learning frequently.* Distance learning requires frequent monitoring and at least weekly communication with the class and timely response to inquiries. Both subject universities have an "Announcements" section of general information as it arises within the Web interface for the class. Here, faculty post something every week, including caveats to get on track with group projects. Most faculty have a posting forum for questions and answers, where student questions are addressed.

Encourage students to e-mail concerns about personal issues. Venting about the group experience will surface here. We visit the group posting pages about every two weeks and send an e-mail to the group applauding their progress or nudging them from lethargy. While many groups will elect the ease of e-mail over these posting forums, we encourage students to use the forum because it allows us to converse with the entire group at once.

There is the unfortunate expectation with electronic forums that feedback will be immediate. Most respondents make it clear that they monitor but do not respond to every submission as it occurs. However, the key to successful communication is to convey the feeling of availability and to develop a rapport. Such relationships pay benefits in academic integrity (Mercuri, 1998).

Principle Four: Evaluate Consistently

• *Weekly or biweekly assessment.* The group project is one assessment. A culture of assessment arises through application of standards throughout the course. Frequent performance assessments provide students with the opportunity to grow accustomed to the grading expectations of the instructor. At every opportunity, the student should see the relationship between the grade received and the work completed. This is common practice in evaluation situations. As a faculty, we should allow for growth and development, and this happens only when the student is provided with feedback more often than at end-of-term submissions.

• *Checklists.* Some faculty members use a grading checklist or heuristics provided through course prefatory materials. These components— perhaps writing, the research component, the contribution to the study projects, and creativity and critical thinking—fairly match the prologue to grading provided above. Weighting of the elements varies.

Principle Five: Evaluate the Many as One

• *The group performs as a group and earns as a group.* As it is in life, individual frustrations will surface regarding perceptions of group performance or cohesiveness. If an excellent student feels trapped by the mediocrity of the group's performance, then the student can shoulder the burden of revising the project as either group facilitator or volunteering to revisit the project to assist. All projects should be subject in draft to a final reading by the group.

One way to diminish the potential impact of the group project on an excellent student's chance at an A is to reduce the value of the group project in the grading scheme. My preference is that the group project serves duty to no more than 25 percent of the student's total class assessment. Thus, a B (80 percent) reflects a loss of 5 points against a course total of 100 points, and a C (70 percent) reflects a loss of 7.5 points. A strong student can shoulder this single devaluation of his or her term work.

• *Student-driven group assessment opportunities.* Many colleagues provide students with the opportunity to evaluate their group project peers. Although I am in the minority on this issue, my view regards this as a shift in burden from the professional evaluator to student, who is less likely to have an objective view of the group process. At times, I do allow students to assess a general discussion conference after I have completed grading but before I have posted grades. This exercise allows students to experience assessment without any effect on their grade. Interjudge reliability on such exercises never musters unanimity. Rarely do students' own meaningful agreement with peers or with their faculty evaluator on class performance outcomes.

Knowledge of a peer review process among group members possibly serves as an internal check on performance. Students disgruntled with a particular member might use such an instrument to vent their frustrations or roust their peers. There is evidence to suggest this is especially true in male evaluations of female members of the group (Falchikov and Magin, 1997). I do not believe a faculty member can value such internal assessments in constructing assessment outcomes. A Supreme Court case argued in late 2001 on the practice of student grading of student work in elementary schools casts a cautious shadow over this approach to assessment (Toppo, 2001). (The Court ruled in 2002 that peer grading did not violate the privacy of educational records.) The student does not share the expertise of the instructor and should not have knowledge of that student's performance, even though it may be casually obvious to them. It is the instructor or his or her own contemporaries who most fairly judge performance. Students are more likely to assess along social variables than performance. The instructor who occasionally witnesses the group's performance and encourages communication with him or her directly will more quickly discern the problems.

Conclusion

The survey research reported in this chapter pointed to five principles for assessment of on-line group performance:

Principle One: Thoroughly Structure the Project. The project is well defined with broad opportunities for original research. Suspense dates are set for accomplishing various components of the project, including opportunities for the group to review drafts before submitting it for final evaluation.

Principle Two: Construct the Groups and Match Membership. Group membership should proportionally mimic the demographics of the class. Assignments should be random otherwise.

Principle Three: Monitor and Communicate Effectively. Feedback should be routine and regular. Students need to develop a rapport with their instructors. Effective communication always begs the question, "Did I address your concerns? Please let me know."

Principle Four: Evaluate Consistently. Instructors should apply the standards defined in Principle One and provide critical feedback on the submissions throughout the term so as to create normative expectations for performance.

Principle Five: Evaluate the Many as One. The group receives one grade for its project. The uses of self-assessments or peer review are not encouraged.

Group assessment is an important component of the students' overall course achievement. The group experience provides opportunities for students to discover strategies for collaborative scholarship, as well as develop avenues for social exchange that are found in traditional classroom environments. Group assessment standards should mirror the assessment experience found throughout the course and be a reflection of the learning culture expectations of the university.

References

Compton, D. M., and Metheny, B. "An Assessment of Grade Inflation in Higher Education." *Perceptual and Motor Skills,* April 2000, *90*(2), 527–537.

Falchikov, N., and Magin, D. "Detecting Gender Bias in Peer Marking of Students' Group Process Work." *Assessment and Evaluation in Higher Education,* 1997, *22*(4), 385–396.

Fay, N., Garrod, S., and Carletta, J. "Group Discussion as Interactive Dialogue or as Serial Monologue: The Influence of Group Size." *Psychological Science,* Nov. 2000, *11*(6), 481.

Haertel, E. "Performance Assessment and Education Reform." *Phi Delta Kappan,* 1999, *80*(9), 662–666.

Janis, I. *Victims of Groupthink.* Boston: Houghton Mifflin, 1972.

Kerridge, J. R., and Mathews, B. "Student Rating of Courses in HE: Further Challenges and Opportunities." *Assessment and Evaluation in Higher Education,* 1998, *73*(1), 71–82.

Laird, E. "Internet Plagiarism: We All Pay the Price." *Chronicle of Higher Education,* July 13, 2001, p. B5.

Lawler, P. A. "Grade Inflation, Democracy, and the Ivy League." *Perspectives on Political Science,* Summer 2001, *30*(3), 133.

Marsh, H. W., and Roche, L. A. "Effects of Grading Leniency and Low Workload on Students' Evaluations of Teaching: Popular Myth, Bias, Validity, or Innocent Bystanders?" *Journal of Educational Psychology,* March 2000, *92*(1), 202–229.

McCarroll, C. "Beating Web Cheats at Their Own Game." *Christian Science Monitor,* Aug. 28, 2001, p. 16.

Mercuri, R. "In Search of Academic Integrity." *Association for Computing Machinery,* 1998, *41*(5), 136.

Prahalad, C. K., and Ramaswamy, V. "The Collaboration Continuum." *Optimize,* Nov. 2001, pp. 31–39.

Race, P. "SEDA Specials": SEDA Induction Pack 1." *Assessment and Evaluation in Higher Education,* 1998, 23(1), 86–88.

Reynolds, M., and Trehan, K. "Assessment: A Critical Perspective." *Studies in Higher Education,* 2000, 25(3), 267–278.

Toppo, G. "High Court Reviews Grading Practice." July 9, 2001. [http://fyi.cnn.com/2001/fyi/teachers.ednews/07/09/grading.papers.ap/index.html]

Weisband, S., and Atwater, L. "Evaluating Self and Others in Electronic and Face-to-Face Groups." *Journal of Applied Psychology,* Aug. 1999, *84*(4), 632–640.

JOHN A. NICOLAY is the director of technology and planning for the Culpeper County (Virginia) Public Schools and professor with the University of Maryland University College, where he teaches on-line within the master's of information technology management program.

6

The movement toward on-line learning presents challenges for professional preparation programs where field experiences are a traditional part of the course of study. Can professors effectively monitor and assess real-world experiences using the Internet?

Assessing Field Experiences

Jane B. Puckett, Rebecca S. Anderson

One result of higher education's growing use of the Internet is a nationwide movement toward on-line teaching (Institute for Higher Education Policy, 2000). According to the National Center for Educational Statistics, one-third of the nation's two-year and four-year postsecondary institutions offered distance education courses during the 1997–98 academic year, with an additional one-fifth of the institutions polled planning to offer such a course within the next three years (U.S. Department of Education, 1999).

This movement toward on-line course work is especially promising and challenging for disciplines with field experiences as a traditional part of the program (Anderson and Puckett, 2001). These real-world learning experiences give students the opportunity to put theory into practice and anchor their developing beliefs (Linek and others, 1999). How can an effective field experience component be integrated with distance learning in professional preparation programs such as nursing, social work, and education? More specifically, how can such a field experience be successfully monitored and assessed by those charged with such responsibilities? If instructors are not present to observe and evaluate these field experiences personally, how do they know what feedback to give students or how to grade their work?

Our experience with on-line technology and field experience involved two classes of teacher education students who posted lesson plans and self and peer responses on a Web site as a component of a graduate-level course in reading education. These students tutored children off-campus to meet a course requirement. One rationale for this assignment is our belief that teachers who are taught on-line will learn to use technology as a communication tool for themselves and employ it in their own classroom with students (Anderson and Speck, 2000; Dooling and Case, 1997; Grisham, 1997;

Leu and Leu, 1997; Riel, Schwartz, and Peterson, 2000). Our job as professors was to monitor students' progress, provide feedback, and assess their field experience by assigning a final grade. We found little information in the literature to support our efforts in assessing this nontraditional, unsupervised clinical environment. The data from our study led us to reflect on the practice of on-line field experience assessment and assisted us in developing a rubric that can be applied to students involved in field experiences in a variety of disciplines.

How We Designed and Assessed On-Line Field Experience

Our institution is a large urban university in the South that regularly provides postgraduate evening courses for students currently in the workplace. The classes we taught, two graduate-level reading courses for students already serving in the teaching field, were structured to meet three hours every other week at the university; on the alternate week, the students met on-line for chapter discussions. Courseinfo, published by Blackboard, was the software package used for on-line communication. In addition, students were required to tutor for one and a half hours a week, lead an on-line discussion forum that corresponded to chapter topics in the required class text, conduct a sixty-minute in-service presentation (part of which was computer generated) on a best teaching practice, and compile a portfolio that demonstrated their learning in the course.

The assessment of the field experience component focused on the students' tutoring. As noted above, the students tutored a child or small group of children in their school or school of choice for one and a half hours a week (one session for ninety minutes or two sessions for forty-five minutes). The students were responsible for assisting the children in developing reading strategies, using the computer, publishing a book or magazine, and developing a computer-based presentation for parents.

Each week, the students posted their lesson plans and responses to their teaching to the class Web site. During the first semester, a rubric (see Exhibit 6.1) was used for self, peer, and teacher responses. In lieu of the rubric, the second-semester class posted an open-ended response journal entry (see Exhibit 6.2) after each lesson. Each Monday, the rubrics or response journal entries were posted on the Web site, and a peer responded by Friday. In addition, a maximum of three lessons were videotaped and exchanged in class for peer review. One tape was then submitted for professor review.

Lessons Learned

Despite challenges, we continue to find much promise in assessing student field experiences on-line. Our study leads us to believe that it can be a positive experience for both students and professors when certain elements are in place:

Exhibit 6.1. Clinical Experience Rubric

Teacher: _____ No. of Students: _____ Name of Responder: _____

Date of Teaching: _____ Date of Response: _____

Is this response for your lesson plan or video? _____

Directions: Indicate the extent to which each of the following is present in the lesson.
0 = Not Observed, 1 = Rarely, 2 = Occasionally, 3 = Frequently, 4 = Extensively

		0	1	2	3	4
Instructional Orientation						
Small Group	_____	❏	❏	❏	❏	❏
One-to-one Tutoring	_____	❏	❏	❏	❏	❏
Computer-Assisted Instruction	_____	❏	❏	❏	❏	❏
Best Teaching Practices						
Reading Aloud	_____	❏	❏	❏	❏	❏
Shared Reading	_____	❏	❏	❏	❏	❏
Guided Reading	_____	❏	❏	❏	❏	❏
Independent Reading	_____	❏	❏	❏	❏	❏
Writing Opportunities/Instruction	_____	❏	❏	❏	❏	❏
Skill Instruction	_____	❏	❏	❏	❏	❏
Instructional Delivery						
Uses higher-level questioning strategies	_____	❏	❏	❏	❏	❏
Has appropriate materials and supplies ready to use	_____	❏	❏	❏	❏	❏
Develops lessons to match students' needs	_____	❏	❏	❏	❏	❏
Uses instructional time effectively and efficiently	_____	❏	❏	❏	❏	❏
Implements purposeful and meaningful tasks	_____	❏	❏	❏	❏	❏
Provides mini lessons	_____	❏	❏	❏	❏	❏
Environment (video only)						
Establishes rapport	_____	❏	❏	❏	❏	❏
Creates supportive physical environment	_____	❏	❏	❏	❏	❏
Challenges students in a positive manner	_____	❏	❏	❏	❏	❏
Uses appropriate verbal and nonverbal communication	_____	❏	❏	❏	❏	❏
Student Assessment						
Conducts diagnostic evaluation	_____	❏	❏	❏	❏	❏
Provides timely and constructive feedback	_____	❏	❏	❏	❏	❏
Communicates progress to students, their parents, or appropriate others	_____	❏	❏	❏	❏	❏

1 = Low, 2 = Moderate, 3 = High

		1	2	3
Summary Items				
Student's level of attention/interest/engagement	_____	❏	❏	❏
Teacher uses best teaching practices	_____	❏	❏	❏
Student employs learned reading/writing strategies	_____	❏	❏	❏
Student instruction is tied to assessment	_____	❏	❏	❏

In addition, please list strengths and concerns.

Strengths:

Concerns:

Exhibit 6.2. Response Journal Entry

Directions: Please reflect on your teaching session and complete the following. Attach your lesson plan with this journal entry.

Name: _____

Students tutored: _____

Date: _____

What went well in the session:

What I could have done differently:

What I learned about my student(s):

What I learned about my teaching:

What I have planned for next week:

What questions I have:

- *Assessment procedures need to be delineated and communicated up front to students.* Precourse organization by the professor is essential to the success of the on-line assessment component. The course Web site must be structured and operational before the first class session, so that students are aware of course expectations and can be shown how to post to the Web site. Students should be assigned a partner or provided an opportunity to choose a partner. The partner provides assessment responses for each assignment. Students also need an assessment time line that lists deadlines for posting self and partner assessments and states when to expect feedback from the partner and professor. The forms used for communication and assessment (such as rubrics and response journal formats) must be accessible on the Web for students from the beginning of the course, so that they structure their field experiences to reflect the assessments. We recommend that the class meet on campus for the first two or three weeks to ensure that students understand the course requirements and procedures and develop a sense of community with the professor and their peers.

- *Before students can reflect on field experiences and offer partner feedback, the professor needs to be sure the students are secure with the technology and know how to get assistance.* The protocol for accessing the course Web site should be given in hard copy to the students for reference. We provided an opportunity for students to log on under our direction during the first class session to check their understanding of the procedures. Even so, several students experienced technical problems accessing the Web site during the first few weeks of the course. The professor needs to be cognizant that difficulties may occur and understand that these problems are to be expected in the early stages of on-line use (Edens, 2000; Grisham, 1997). Students need a plan for seeking technical assistance if problems arise. We encouraged students to e-mail or telephone us if they were experiencing on-line problems. Students could also call the University Technical Support Hotline for help. If students experience technical difficulties and there is no assistance, the on-line component will quickly become a source of stress and frustration.

- *The professor must model for students all the procedures that will be used to assess field experiences.* Field experiences can be communicated on-line in much the same way they were traditionally recorded by including such items as goals, objectives, strategies, activities, procedures, interventions, assessments, future plans, and recommendations. In our case, each student tutored a child and completed a lesson plan for each session. The lesson plan followed an open-ended format that asked students to fill in a narrative description of their purpose for teaching, strategies and activities employed, tutor response and assessment, and materials used. The professor is responsible for modeling the format that will be used to communicate the field experience and give examples of items that should be included in the explanation. Then the professor must model appropriate feedback for the described field experience—not only the format for this feedback but also the language and tone. It is important that students understand how to reflect on their own field experience and that of peers in a constructive way.

• *Student reflection is a primary goal of field experiences.* In a constructivist paradigm, we strive to develop reflective students who are able to guide their learning and construct their own meaning. With this in mind, the reflection portion of the field experience becomes its most important aspect. The professor is responsible for emphasizing the value of student reflection and providing a model for cognition involved in this process with his or her own feedback to students. In our study, students were required to reflect on their own teaching and the teaching of a partner, and then we provided feedback on their lessons. All student and professor responses remained on the Web site throughout the semester, accessible to all class members for reference.

• *There are benefits and problems associated with the use of a rubric for the assessment of field experiences.* One assessment tool available for student reflection and professor feedback is a rubric. When designing a rubric, the professor delineates the points that are essential to the students' field experiences so that the rubric serves as a reminder of those items to be included in the field experience. Rubrics can be continually modified to reflect the learning that is taking place by excluding old items and including new ones.

The rubric we used had five categories with subheadings that asked the students and professor to rate, using a number scale from 0 through 5, the extent to which each point was present in the lesson taught (see Exhibit 6.1). We also asked for narrative comments on the strengths and weakness of the teaching. A professor who is interested in expanding the quantitative data from the rubric with additional qualitative information can provide space to reflect in a more open-ended way by allowing for feedback on a particular aspect of the field experience.

We found students to be more comfortable with a qualitative response (journal entry) than a quantitative response (rubric). However, we believe there are things a professor can do to improve the success of a rubric response. If a rubric is going to be used, students need to be actively engaged in its development and modification. This involvement can provide them with a sense of ownership with the evaluation of their learning and give them the opportunity to highlight what they value in their field experience. Students need training in using and scoring the rubric before they are required to employ this assessment tool.

• *There are benefits and problems associated with the use of a journal entry for the assessment of field experiences.* A journal entry provides a qualitative look at field experience in an open-ended narrative format. Questions are posed to the students and serve as a guide for reflection. In our study, the journal entry questions asked what was learned, how the student felt about the session, and what the plans were for the following week (see

Exhibit 6.2). A professor wishing to use a journal entry response to student field experience can modify these questions to meet the needs of particular situations. Again, it is essential that the professor be ready to model what these written responses will contain. One way for the professor to do this is to share reflections on his or her own teaching.

As professors, we found that sometimes students' journal entries did not completely reflect on all aspects of their lessons. Again, the professor needs to model what he or she expects to be included in an entry. A combination of rubric and journal entry seems to be the most effective way for students to reflect on their teaching.

• *Visual augmentation adds a positive dimension to assessing field experiences on-line.* Another way to provide feedback to students is to have them submit videotapes of portions of their field experiences. The tape allows the professor to experience the students' actual off-campus situations and see how they conduct themselves with their participants. With the videotape, the professor can capture the actual experience without the constraints of time or place.

The use of videotapes early on in the field experience is a good source of formative evaluation. It allows the professor to correct misconceptions in the practice before they become learned and provides a clearer understanding of each student's unique field experience. Tapes made later in the field experience provide for summative evaluation. Feedback to students at this point can be in the form of a narrative response or a rubric. In our study, we applied the same rubric or response journal entry used in assessing the field experience posted on-line.

Digital technology is available for posting these tapes on-line along with other artifacts for the course. We are experimenting with this technology and have plans for students to place video clips of their field experience on-line.

• *The professor must recognize the student's need for timely expert feedback.* It is our experience that many students currently serving in the field enroll in university courses to update their knowledge and skills by seeking to learn from professors, whom they view as experts. Because in this case, the field experience is communicated on-line, some students may feel removed from the guidance of the professor, so it is important for the professor to respond on-line to student field experiences in a consistent and timely manner. Just as there is a weekly schedule for students to post their field experiences, there should be expectations in place for professor feedback. Students demand and deserve quality feedback from professors

• *Professors can improve their own practice by reading student reflections.* As students reflect on and improve their practice, we must, as professors, view their reflections as an assessment of our teaching. Student reflections are an excellent source of feedback on the organization and content of the field experience we have provided.

Conclusion

Removing field experience from a clinical setting does not free professors from their traditional roles as monitors and evaluators. It does cause them to rethink the structure and procedures in guiding the field experience. The goal for field experience is to give students a sense of the real world of their discipline and facilitate their lifelong learning. The on-line component provides flexibility for field experience that both student and professor can enjoy. We believe it has merit and can be done in a manner that is beneficial to all concerned.

References

Anderson, R. S., and Puckett, J. B. "In Line with the On-Line Class: Using the Internet for Field Experience Response." Paper presented at the meeting of the National Reading Conference, San Antonio, Tex., 2001.

Anderson, R. S., and Speck, B. W. *Using Technology in K–8 Literacy Classrooms.* Upper Saddle River, N.J.: Prentice Hall, 2000.

Dooling, J. O., and Case, K. I. "Integrating Technology into Teacher Preparation Programs." *Teaching Education,* 1997, *8,* 9–19.

Edens, K. M. "Promoting Communication, Inquiry and Reflections in an Early Practicum Experience via an On-Line Discussion Group." *Action in Teacher Education,* 2000, *22,* 14–23.

Grisham, D. L. "Electronic Literacy Learning: Teachers' On-Line Dialogue Journals." In C. Kinzer, K. Hinchman, and D. Leu (eds.), *Inquiries in Literacy Theory and Practice.* Chicago: National Reading Conference, 1997.

Institute for Higher Education Policy. *Quality on the Line: Benchmarks for Success in Internet-Based Distance Education.* Washington, D.C.: Institute for Higher Education Policy, Apr. 2000.

Leu, D. J., and Leu, D. D. *Teaching with the Internet: Lessons from the Classroom.* Norwood, Mass.: Christopher-Gordon, 1997.

Linek, W. M., and others. "Developing Beliefs About Literacy Instruction: A Cross-Case Analysis of Preservice Teachers in Traditional and Field-Based Settings." *Reading Research and Instruction,* 1999, *38*(4), 371–386.

Riel, M. M., Schwartz, J., and Peterson, H. "The Power of Owning Technology." *Educational Leadership,* 2000, *57*(8), 58–60.

U. S. Department of Education. *Distance Education at Postsecondary Education Institutions: 1997–98.* Washington, D.C.: U.S. Department of Education, 1999.

JANE B. PUCKETT is a doctoral student in the Department of Instruction and Curriculum Leadership at the University of Memphis, Tennessee.

REBECCA S. ANDERSON is the director of Writing Across the Curriculum for the University of Memphis, Tennessee, and an associate professor in the Department of Instruction and Curriculum Leadership.

7

Attention to key concepts, resources, and strategies such as testing and assessment can greatly enhance the ability of on-line curricular offerings to accommodate learners with a wide range of disabilities.

Enhancing On-Line Learning for Individuals with Disabilities

James M. Brown

Kuchinke, Aragon, and Bartlett (2001) noted that it is difficult to imagine a technical innovation with greater potential influence on human performance technology than the Internet and the World Wide Web. They concluded that the design, delivery, and use of instruction over the Internet have yet to be adequately examined, for such instructional efforts are more complex than simply "moving content onto the Web" (p. 19). Other issues, such as how best to promote student learning during on-line instruction, should be examined and assessed. This is especially important when seeking to accommodate the unique learning needs of individuals with disabilities.

Although a seemingly unending stream of Internet-related technologies continues to enhance the speed of access and the quantity of information that are becoming available for on-line learning initiatives, far too little emphasis has been focused on helping all learners interact with these new technologies and the information sources to which they offer access (Djoudi and Harous, 2001).

Given this chapter's focus on on-line learning for individuals with disabilities, it is important to review some of the rationale for such educational activities that are, or will be, enhanced by the use of technology. Blanchard, Cohen, and Curry (2001) suggested that the need for such an

I am grateful to Generating Assistive Technology Systemically (http://genasys.usm .maine.edu), a program at the University of Southern Maine, for its high-quality on-line learning-related resources for learners with disabilities, which I used for much of this chapter's discussion.

effort is supported by a variety of factors. First, it is mandated by the following federal legislation:

Individuals with Disabilities Education Act Amendments of 1997 (IDEA). Requires that individuals who receive scholarship assistance from federal sources intended to help the disabled must complete a service obligation that benefits part of the disabled community or repay all or part of their assistance funds.

Americans with Disabilities Act (ADA), 1990. Wide-ranging legislation intended to make society more accessible. Its five areas include employment, public services, public accommodations, telecommunications, and miscellaneous, which includes prohibitions on threatening or retaliating against disabled persons who are asserting their rights under the ADA.

Rehabilitation Act Amendments of 1998. Section 504 prohibits discrimination in all programs and activities conducted by recipients of federal financial assistance, and section 508 specifies that electronic and information technology developed, procured, maintained, or used by the federal government must be accessible to people with disabilities.

Assistive Technology Act of 1998 (ATA) acknowledges the awareness of benefits of assistive technology interagency coordination.

Educational Accommodations and Modifications

It is clear that many learners with disabilities can and do benefit from technology enhancement of educational programs and services. IDEA does not define accommodations or modifications, but the PACER Center (Parent Advocacy Coalition for Educational Rights, 2001) found general agreement on the following assumptions about the use of these two terms:

> Accommodation. ". . . . allows a student to complete the same assignment or test as other students, but with a change in the timing, formatting, setting, scheduling, response, and/or presentation. This. . . . does not alter in any significant way what the test or assignment measures."
>
> Modification. ". . . . an adjustment to an assignment or a test that changes the standard or what the test or assignment is supposed to measure" [p. 1].

The PACER Center (2001) suggested that asking students what would be helpful for addressing their learning needs is the desired first step in accommodation and modification processes. The PACER Center's Web site (http://www.fape.org) contains extensive lists of accommodations and modifications. PACER includes accommodations and modifications in the categories below that have implications for efforts to address the learning needs of on-line instruction for persons with disabilities. The importance of these efforts is supported by Souza and Dias's conclusion (1996) that on-line learning initiatives that access information on the Web for learners with disabilities (as well as other learners) often encounter typical problems characterized by disorientation and cognitive overload. These problems occur in such areas as textbooks and curriculum, instruction and assignments, and handwriting.

Generating Assistive Technology Systemically (GENASYS), a program at the University of Southern Maine, has developed a wide variety of high-quality on-line learning-related resources for learners with disabilities (http://genasys.usm.maine.edu). In addition, the U.S. Department of Education's program Preparing Teachers to Teach with Technology (PT3) has begun development of a wide range of instructional technology resources that apply to all learners (U.S. Department of Education, 2001). Both of these Internet resources, as well as numerous others, address the unique learning needs of learners with disabilities.

Mehlinger and Powers (2002) concluded that technology, when effectively applied to learners with disabilities, can support such students in "pull-out" programs, as well as enabling learners in "inclusive education programs to participate actively in the general education curriculum and achieve academic success" (p. 154). The widespread use of such instructional resources for all students is a key aspect of the movement to provide "a more inclusive delivery model, referred to as inclusive education or inclusion" (p. 153). This chapter identifies key concepts, practices, and resources related to such efforts aimed at learners with disabilities.

See Exhibit 7.1 for a list of implementation issues related to on-line accommodations.

Assistive Technology

The use of assistive technology is closely related to the design and delivery of on-line instruction for learners with disabilities. GENASYS (2002) defines assistive technology as "any item, piece of equipment, or product system—whether acquired commercially off the shelf, modified, or customized—that is used to increase, maintain, or improve functional capabilities of an individual with a disability." It can be a device or a service.

There are numerous forms and levels of cost and complexity of assistive technology, ranging from low-tech and low-cost to high-tech and higher-cost options.

GENASYS (2002) lists specific examples of assistive technology—for example:
Auditory amplification system
Raised or highlighted graphs or diagrams
Closed-captioned television
Alternative keyboard
Audiotape
Braille
Large print

Exhibit 7.1. Implementation Issues Related to On-Line Accommodations

1. *When should accommodations be used?*
   a. To ensure that an assessment measures the student's knowledge and skills rather than the student's disabilities (e.g., when classroom accommodations are made so that learning is not impeded by a student's disability, such accommodations generally should be provided during assessment).
   b. Accommodations should not be introduced for the first time during an assessment (base decisions about assessment accommodations on what students need in order to be provided with an equal opportunity to show what they know without impediment of their disabilities).
2. *Who makes the decisions about accommodations?*
Most decisions about who needs assessment accommodations should be made by people who know the educational needs of the student. (Federal law now requires that this be the Individualized Education Program (IEP) team, if student has not yet graduated from high school and has not yet reached the age of 22. However, a student's general education teachers can provide input to accommodations decisions—even if they are not members of the IEP team.)
3. *What is the impact of assessment accommodations on score comparability?*
   • Most states and school districts use professional judgment to determine which accommodations affect score comparability.
   • Reading a test aloud to the student when the reading test is measuring decoding generally is considered to change the nature of the task. The resulting score probably should not be compared to other decoding scores.
   • If the test is measuring reading comprehension, reading a test aloud allows the student to demonstrate this skill without the barrier of disability. The resulting score likely could be compared to other students' scores.
4. *How fair is it to provide assessment accommodations to some students, but not others?*
The intent of providing accommodations is to ensure that the test is measuring the student's skills, not just the effects of disability.
5. *How does the type of test (e.g., norm-referenced vs. criterion-referenced) affect assessment accommodation decisions?*
   a. Norm-referenced tests (NRT) are used to allow comparisons to norms developed under standardized procedures.
   b. Criterion-Referenced Tests (CRTs) assess whether students can perform particular tasks, but do not compare a student's performance to a standardization group.
6. *How are accommodated test scores reported?*
   a. When accommodations are used to measure a student's skill, and not the effect of a disability, scores can be aggregated to best capture the performance of all students.
   b. When the effects of particular accommodations are questioned: (a) aggregate the data with the rest of the test scores and (b) disaggregate the scores of students receiving questionable accommodations.
7. *Is an out-of-level test an appropriate accommodation?*
This issue is controversial. When an assessment is used for system accountability purposes, it may not be appropriate to use out-of-level testing because it does not reflect the student's performance relative to the standards being assessed. If the assessment is being used solely for instructional purposes, then out-of-level testing may be appropriate.
8. *What are "Universally Designed Assessments"?*
"Universally designed assessments" are designed and developed to be accessible and valid for the widest range of students, including students with disabilities and students with limited-English proficiency. They are designed so that floor or ceiling effects do not prevent good measurement of all students.

Exhibit 7.1. (Continued)

9. What Types of Testing Accommodations for Students with Disabilities May Be Affected by State Government Policies?
Readers are encouraged to check their specific state's policies regarding the following "allowed" testing accommodation categories:
1. Presentation (e.g., repeat directions, read aloud, use of larger bubbles)
2. Response (e.g., mark answers in book, use reference aids, point)
3. Setting (e.g., study carrel, special lighting, separate room)

Source: GENASYS [http://education.umn.edu/nceo/TopicAreas/Accommodations/Accom_FAQ.htm]

Screen reader (or other text-to-speech devices)
Scanner
Talking calculator
Calculator with large keys or LCD screen
Audio description
Touch screen
Voice recognition
Speech synthesizer
Specialized computer software
Screen reader
Screen enlarger
Text-to-speech
Voice recognition
Word prediction
Conceptual mapping
Word processor

Web Accessibility

GENASYS (2002) points out that "accessible Web design and construction allow all people to join in and benefit from the use of this powerful tool." Suggestions for implementing effective instructional Web sites are provided below.

Quick Tips to Make Accessible Web Sites. Educators developing their own Web-based instruction should guide their ongoing efforts or review their past accomplishments in terms of a wide variety of assessment criteria (GENASYS, 2002):

Images and animations. Supplement all information with textual equivalents wherever possible. Use the .alt tag to describe images.
Image maps. An image map is a graphic divided into one or more areas, with each area pointing to a different URL. Text-based additions to image maps increase their accessibility to people browsing with nongraphical browsers.
Multimedia. Provide captioning and transcripts of audio information and audio descriptions of video information.

Hypertext links. Use text that makes sense when read out of context. For instance, do not use "click here."

Web page organization. Use headings, lists, and consistent structure.

Graphs and charts. Summarize graphics and charts by providing a link to a textual explanation of the information provided in those graphics and charts.

Scripts, applets, and plug-ins. Applets are programs that are automatically downloaded and run on the user's machine. Provide an alternative content format in case these features are inaccessible or unsupported by the user's computer system.

Tables. Avoid using tables. Most screen readers read across the page, reading data and sentences on the same row from different columns as one sentence. Provide a summary of the table's structure and purpose.

Blanchard, Cohen, and Curry (2001) provide a useful discussion of efforts to apply assistive technologies to enhance the effectiveness of learning for all students. In analyzing the assistive technology needs of individual learners, they suggest that instructors ask the following questions:

- What are the student's strengths?
- What learning tasks are difficult for the student?
- What environment is the student working in when the difficulty is present?
- What strategies or tools have been successful in the past with this student?
- Has assistive technology been used before?
- Has the student shown an interest in technology?

A number of assistive technology devices can be used to improve learning outcomes—for example:

Touch window	Adaptive keyboard
Augmentative communication device	Switch
Head pointer	Key guard
Slant board	Pencil grip

The capabilities of the computer, keyboard, and mouse themselves can be adapted to fit various disabilities:

Magnification (visual)
Contrast (visual, cognitive)
Toggle keys (visual)
Hot keys (mobility)
Mouse keys (mobility)
Filter keys (single-handed typing or weak fine motor skills)
Character repeat settings (single-handed typing or weak fine motor skills)

Sticky keys (single-handed typing, mouth or head stick, hunting and peck-
   ing)
Clicking speed (mobility, cognitive developmental issues)
Pointer appearance (visual impairments, cognitive developmental issues)
Pointer speed (visual impairment, cognitive developmental issues)
Pointer tail (visual impairment, cognitive developmental issues)
Right or left mouse switch (individual student use)

The following factors are important to address when seeking to maximize Web site accessibility by all learners:

- People access the Web in very different ways.
- Web sites should be designed in ways that enable access by all people.
- Emerging technologies are supported by accessible Web site design.

The Impact of Web Sites with Limited Accessibility. Learners with
disabilities represent a substantial component of the learner population;
they comprise approximately 15 percent of the school-age population and
represent approximately 25 percent of the entire U.S. population. Improved
Web site design efforts could be of benefit to persons who must function
within the following constraints:

May not be able to see, hear, move, or be able to process some types of
   information easily or at all
May not have or be able to use a keyboard or mouse
May have difficulty reading or comprehending text

Conclusion

Improved development of and access to effective on-line learning resources
is an issue that all educators, especially those focused on the learning needs
and resources of individuals with disabilities, should address. An increasing array of support resources for such priorities is continuing to emerge.
Readers are encouraged to seek out these resources and to apply them to
their efforts to educate all learners whom they serve.

References

Blanchard, D., Cohen, L., and Curry, C. (2001). "Using Technology to Improve Learning
   Outcomes for All Students." PT3 Catalyst Grant, University of Southern Maine, 2001.
   [http://genasys.usm.maine. edu/workshop/pt3_8201.ppt].
Djoudi, M., and Harous, S. "Simplifying the Learning Process over the Internet." *T.H.E.
   Journal,* Nov. 2001.
Generating Assistive Technology Systemically (GENASYS). "Web Accessibility
   Resources." [http://genasys.usm. maine.edu/access.htm]. 2002.

Kuchinke, K. P., Aragon, S. R., and Bartlett, K. R. "On-Line Instructional Delivery: Lessons from the Instructor's Perspective." *Performance Improvement,* 2001, *40,* 19–27.

Mehlinger, H., and Powers, S. *Technology and Teacher Education.* Boston: Houghton Mifflin, 2001.

PACER Center. "Families and Advocates Partnership for Education: School Accommodations and Modifications." Minneapolis: PACER Center, Sept. 2001.

Souza, A., and Dias, P. *Analysis of Hypermedia Browsing Process in Order to Reduce Disorientation.* Proceedings of ED-MEDIA 96 and ED-TELECOM 96 Conference (Boston, June 17–22, 1996). Charlottesville, Va.: Association for the Advancement of Computing in Education, 1996.

U.S. Department of Education. *Preparing Tomorrow's Teachers to Use Technology.* Washington, D.C.: U.S. Government Printing Office, 2001. [http://www.PT3.org].

JAMES M. BROWN *is a professor of work, community, and family education in the College of Education and Human Development at the University of Minnesota, St. Paul.*

8

Once they are aware of both the promises and pitfalls of e-folios, professors can make effective use of these collections of student work to enhance their students' learning and facilitate their own process of responding to student work.

Assessing E-Folios in the On-Line Class

Mark Canada

"I love being a writer," Peter De Vries said of his profession. "What I can't stand is the paperwork" (Peter, 1977, p. 541). Many professors have had the same thought, especially when the first wave of student essays inundates their offices. The problem is worse for those more ambitious professors who have joined the movement toward portfolios. Now, in addition to periodic storms of drafts, they also must brace themselves for the hurricane of final portfolios that strike at semester's end, swamp their offices, and linger on desks and spare chairs like floodwaters that refuse to abate. Even on-line professors, who may never exchange a single sheet of paper with their students, must cope with blizzards of e-mail messages, chatroom discussions, and postings on discussion forums.

In recent years, professors of both on-line and traditional classes have witnessed the introduction of electronic portfolios, or e-folios, an innovation that not only provides relief from paperwork but promises significant pedagogical benefits. E-folios are collections of student work stored in digital format—on a CD-ROM, for example, or in the form of an Internet site. In addition to carrying the same advantages that experts have associated with their traditional counterparts, such as a greater emphasis on revision, an improved relationship between professor and student, and emphasis on issues regarding audience (Elbow and Belanoff, 1991), e-folios extend these benefits and offer some of their own. E-folios, for example, have unique navigational advantages, are generally easier to maintain and share than their traditional counterpart, and encourage the development of additional communication skills.

To make the most of these benefits while minimizing the effects of a few pitfalls, professors interested in using e-folios must make educated decisions about format, implementation, and evaluation.

Format

In any assessment situation, professors must first decide exactly what they wish to evaluate, which depends on what they wish their students to learn. An advantage of traditional portfolios is that they expand the scope of material that students can use to demonstrate their growth and competence (Yancey, 1996). Instead of submitting three essays and taking a final exam, a student might turn in a portfolio that contains drafts, essays, photocopies of sources, and even photographs and audiotapes or videotapes. At the least, portfolios often include reflective essays in which students discuss their growth and refer to other materials in the portfolio.

E-folios extend this advantage. Whereas traditional portfolios require an elaborate system of appendixes and cross-references, e-folios allow students to integrate text and other elements, including photographs, illustrations, diagrams, charts, and audio and video recordings (Milone, 1995). For instance, a student's lab report might include a verbal description, a diagram, and a video recording (Niguidula, 1997). By using links judiciously, students can guide professors and other readers through their portfolios. Each of my students' portfolios, for example, includes an index page, a kind of cover page that features the student's name and e-mail address, as well as a brief profile and a table of contents featuring links to every component of the e-folio. Anyone visiting this e-folio can quickly and easily go directly to any component. Students also can use links to connect their reflective essays and captions to illustrative examples. A composition student reflecting on his or her progress in the area of using sources, for instance, might include links to examples of effective source use in several essays.

Once they have decided what they wish students to include in their e-folios, professors need to consider the format. CD-ROM has been a favorite format among many institutions, including Wright State University in Dayton, Ohio, and public schools in Indianapolis (Wiedmer, 1998). Wiedmer notes that this format offers significant advantages in the areas of price and ease of use, although burning several CDs in order to update information can be expensive and time-consuming. Some professors may choose to have students store their e-folios on hard drives or campus networks (Lankes, 1998). Professors can use software programs, such as Aurbach's Grady Profile and Roger Wagner Publishing's HyperStudio, to give their students templates for their e-folios (Lankes, 1998; Milone, 1995).

Yet another format is the on-line portfolio, which each student maintains in the form of his or her own World Wide Web site. To maintain this type of e-folio, students need to reserve space on a server, such as the one maintained by Geocities (www.geocities.com), which allows anyone to publish as much as 15 megabytes of information for free in exchange for the right to post small advertisements on each Web page. Some professors may want to consider having students publish their pages on their own university's server, although students may have to move these pages after they graduate. Students then use Web-authoring software to build their pages, finally publishing these pages to their server. Professors may want to require students to use a particular software package for building their pages so that they can offer technical assistance. I use Netscape Composer, which is already available on our university's computers, is free to download at home, and is easy to use.

On-line e-folios offer distinct advantages over traditional portfolios, as well as e-folios stored on CD-ROMs, hard drives, or campus networks. Unlike those stored in three-ring binders or on CD-ROMs, on-line portfolios are easy and inexpensive to update, encouraging students to revise their work often and extensively. Students who maintain on-line portfolios may be more likely to view their work as a constant candidate for revision—as professional writers and designers do with a work in progress. Furthermore, no matter how many revisions they undergo, on-line e-folios look perpetually polished.

On-line portfolios are also more accessible than other kinds of e-folios, being available twenty-four hours a day to the professor, classmates, and indeed anyone else with access to the Internet. Although this accessibility might be problematic in cases where students' postings are personal, it frees the professor from managing piles of notebooks or CD-ROMS and opens up several pedagogical opportunities, especially for professors of on-line courses. In one such course I taught, "Introduction to Literature," I encouraged the students to read one another's on-line portfolios to learn about the course material. By simulating class discussion, their e-folios emphasized student-centered learning. Furthermore, since I assigned research essays on objective information, such as the history of Robin Hood, along with essays involving literary interpretation, these e-folios also relieved some of the burden on me to prepare and transmit course material over the Internet. In a Web-enhanced composition course, I took this concept a step further and encouraged students to use one another's on-line portfolios as sources for their own research articles. On-line e-folios also enable professors and students to conduct draft workshops without ever meeting in the classroom. Finally, after the course ends, students can continue to maintain their portfolios on the Web, using them to demonstrate their abilities to graduate schools or potential employers.

In short, on-line e-folios allow students to keep their best foot constantly forward, allowing them to revise continually and make clean, polished products available to millions of people all over the world. My students feel a unique sense of pride in their e-folios, showing them off to friends and relatives.

Implementation

Having decided on a format for their students' e-folios, professors need to develop a plan for implementing them in their courses. Like those who assign traditional portfolios, for example, these professors must decide how many components will go into their students' e-folios, what types of components they will require or encourage—essays, drafts, photographs, recordings, and so on—how many revisions they will allow, what strategies they will use to help students develop their portfolios, and how much weight the entire portfolio will carry in students' final course grades. When making these decisions, professors should consider some possibilities and pitfalls of e-folios.

In some respects, e-folios expand the possibilities for the kinds of materials that students can use to demonstrate their growth and competence. E-folios allow relatively easy integration of text and other elements, such as photographs and recordings, and professors may want to mandate or recommend certain components. However, e-folios are not entirely conducive to some types of artifacts, such as handwritten notes and photocopies of sources. If professors wish to view such materials, they can require students to convert them into a digital format by scanning them. Because such a process can be tedious, professors might simply require students to keep hard copies and supply them on request. If the student is not local, the professor must leave time for such material to travel through the mail.

Unlike traditional portfolios, e-folios call for special equipment (Niguidula, 1997; Milone, 1995). Making sure that students have access to this equipment, as well as the skills to use it, can be a challenge in on-line courses, where students may be logging in from very different locales. Thus, professors may want to require only components that students can produce with an average home computer—verbal essays, links to Internet sites, and perhaps illustrations—though they still may accept other types of material, such as photographs and recordings, from students who have access to the necessary hardware and software.

A greater challenge is ensuring that students have the skills they need to assemble their on-line portfolios (Purvis, 1996). I have tried a number of strategies to help students acquire these skills. For example, I post detailed instructions on my Web site and link them to the unit plans for the course. In my Web-enhanced courses, I devote at least one class session to showing students how to reserve Web space, build a Web page, and publish it. In on-line courses, I cover this material in optional training sessions. Some students in these courses have attended these sessions, and others have simply used my instructions to train themselves. I also provide students with one-on-one assistance by e-mail, telephone, and face-to-face conferences.

Although the process of building and maintaining an on-line e-folio is relatively simple and can be learned in about an hour, many students inevitably struggle at the outset. Merely typing "www" instead of "ftp" can keep them from publishing their work, and because the concepts of links and subdirectories may be alien to them, many students cannot do their own troubleshooting at first. For this reason, professors who assign e-folios should be prepared to spend several hours troubleshooting with students during the first few weeks of a course. To provide an incentive for students to master the necessary skills early, professors may want to set an early deadline for the first component of the portfolio. In a typical course, I require students to publish their index page at the end of the first week of classes

Assessment

When it comes to assessment, e-folios resemble their traditional counterparts. Professors may decide to evaluate only the final portfolio or to grade individual components over the course of the semester and then assign a separate grade to the final portfolio. Furthermore, they may elect to assign points to various assignments or simply assess the entire portfolio holistically. In any case, professors will want to use a rubric that refers to standard criteria, such as accuracy and creativity, and to share this rubric with students at the beginning of the semester. Because of the nature of this medium, they may also want to take into consideration a few other aspects, such as appearance and ease of navigation. For example, my evaluation criteria state that projects should be accurate, clear, and readable but also functional and attractive. If professors include such considerations in their criteria, they should provide not only technical assistance with setting up links and changing colors, but also guidance on general principles of graphic design. In my composition courses, I include a unit on graphic communication, in which I cover font selection, focal points, and related concepts.

Students who are creating e-folios, then, have to demonstrate additional skills on top of those required for traditional essays and portfolios. Professors can encourage students to view such "extra" requirements not as burdens but as opportunities. As on-line communication is becoming the norm, links and graphic elements are important communication tools in their own right, and knowing how to use them effectively is akin to knowing how to organize a paragraph or paraphrase a source.

Professors accustomed to circling words and writing in margins will need to devise new methods for responding to their students' e-folios. Of course, they still can write general comments, either saving them directly on the hard drive with the e-folio itself or sending them to the student as an e-mail message. Marking and commenting on specific passages is only slightly more complicated. If the original essay was saved as a Microsoft Word document, for example, the professor can type comments in a different typeface in the text itself (Howard, 1996) or use the convenient "insert comment" function to highlight passages and respond to them. If students are publishing on-line portfolios, the professor may download each essay, type comments directly onto it, save the essay, and return it to the student on a diskette or as an e-mail attachment.

With some ingenuity and preparation, professors can use the electronic environment to facilitate responding to students' work. Howard (1996) describes an "electronic boilerplate" she uses to respond to a particular common problem she encounters in student portfolios. For my classes, I have created an electronic evaluation form with links to Web pages I have created on core concepts, such as research, drafting, and revision. If the portfolio shows problems in one of these areas, I list it under "Areas of Improvement" and e-mail the form to the student as an attachment. The student then can click on the link to find guidance for revising the portfolio.

I evaluate my students' on-line portfolios at least twice during the semester. First, in the weeks before midterm, I visit each student's on-line portfolio, cut the major contents, and paste them onto an evaluation form that I have created. At the top of this form, I type some general comments

Exhibit 8.1. Evaluation Criteria for E-Folios

Content
The portfolio must contain all the assignments described on the syllabus. Each individual project in the portfolio should thoroughly and insightfully address its subject with accurate, credible, timely, and relevant information. Argumentative essays should state clear, substantive, contestable, and precise claims early and support these claims with appropriate evidence.

Clarity
Each written project in the portfolio should present information in a clear, logical fashion. In general, each paragraph in the written projects generally should begin with a precise topic sentence, followed by clear, well-organized sentences that support the topic sentence. Transitional words and phrases should effectively guide the audience through the information.

Style
All work should engage the audience with lively, concise writing and should generally lack lapses in tone, register, punctuation, mechanics, spelling, word choice, and grammar. Each project should effectively incorporate source material with proper use of attribution, paraphrases, and quotations. Longer projects should begin with engaging introductions and include satisfying conclusions. Written projects should be functional and attractive, conforming to all appropriate professional standards. In particular, all parenthetical citations and lists of works cited in the written projects should conform to MLA [Modern Language Association] style.

Integrity
Each project must be your own work. That is, except for properly cited quotations, every sentence and phrase must be in your own words. All interpretations, except for those properly cited, also must be your own. If you turn in someone else's work, use a source's exact words without placing these words in quotation marks, or use an interpretation you found in a source without giving credit to the source, you are guilty of plagiarism and may fail this course. You must be prepared to prove that you have done all your own work by showing or mailing me your sources and discussing the details of your project with me in conference, either in person or over the telephone.

in the form of a letter. At the bottom, where I have pasted the student's essays, I insert comments, questions, and suggestions. This evaluation form also includes notes on areas for improvement, each linked to a Web site with helpful hints, and a tentative grade that reflects the quality of the portfolio at that point. Students then have the rest of the semester to revise their portfolios, using my evaluation forms to revise their existing work and construct strong future work. Near the end of the semester, I evaluate the entire portfolio again, now in its finished form, and assign a final grade. On each occasion, I use a holistic approach, assigning a grade that reflects the student's overall mastery of course content.

Exhibit 8.1 sets out the criteria I use in my Web-enhanced courses. Using criteria such as these, I evaluate each student's portfolio holistically and assign a grade that reflects his or her overall mastery of course content.

Conclusion

Professors striving to provide students with the best on-line educational experiences can capitalize on the possibilities of the technology and look for ways to adapt proven strategies from traditional classrooms. Portfolios may provide students with extra incentives to revise their work, increase their sense of ownership, and foster their relationships with their professors. E-folios provide and extend these benefits, encouraging on-line students to revise even more often, giving them an even greater sense of pride, facilitating draft workshops and other forms of interchange, and saving on-line professors a lot of paperwork in the process.

References

Elbow, P., and Belanoff, P. "State University of New York at Stony Brook Portfolio-Based Evaluation Program." In P. Belanoff and M. Dickson (eds.), *Portfolios: Process and Product.* Portsmith, N.H.: Boynton Cook, 1991.

Howard, R. "Memoranda to Myself: Maxims for the On-Line Portfolio." *Computers and Composition,* 1996, *13*(2), 155–167.

Lankes, A. "Portfolios: A New Wave in Assessment." *T.H.E. Journal,* 1998, *25*(9), 18–19.

Milone, M. "Electronic Portfolios: Who's Doing Them and How?" *Technology and Learning,* 1995, *16*(2), 28–33.

Niguidula, D. "Picturing Performance with Digital Portfolios." *Educational Leadership,* 1997, *55*(3), 26–29.

Peter, L. J. *Peter's Quotations.* New York: Bantam, 1977.

Purvis, A. "Electronic Portfolios." *Computers and Composition,* 1996, *13*(2), 135–146.

Wiedmer, T. "Digital Portfolios." *Phi Delta Kappan,* 1998, *79*(8), 586–590.

Yancey, K. "Portfolio, Electronic, and the Links Between." *Computers and Composition,* 1996, *13*(2), 129–133.

MARK CANADA is an assistant professor of English at the University of North Carolina at Pembroke, where he teaches on-line and Web-enhanced courses.

9

Professors with limited technological expertise or resources can use features of their existing computer networks, such as e-mail and Web postings, to communicate assessment expectations to their on-line students.

Preparing Students for Assessment in the On-Line Class

Michele L. Ford

In traditional classrooms, students are plagued with questions and concerns regarding assessment: "What are the instructions for section two again?" "How do we know what answer you're looking for on question five?" "I don't understand how I got this grade." In on-line classes, the same dilemmas appear more problematic. For example, Monaghan (1996) reports that some practitioners fear technology will never compensate for the understated elements of human interpersonal interaction when professors communicate with students. Indeed, cyberlearning is couched in an apparent paradox of twenty-four-hour access to the professor over the Internet but the absence of customary face-to-face interaction. This leaves room for open speculation whether it is more difficult in on-line classes than in face-to-face classes to apprise students of assessment expectations. However, with the availability and efficiency of electronic communication, traditional and on-line courses can be very similar (Canada, 2000). For example, a fundamental component of both successful face-to-face and on-line classes is assessment, so it is not surprising that successful on-line programs pay careful attention to assessment. Carnevale (2001), for instance, describes how some of the nation's virtual universities use highly advanced outcomes-based assessment policies, including administering a battery of pre- and posttests to measure students' proficiency.

Because of the concern about and development of assessment policies and measures for on-line classes, some predict that on-line evaluation will become the prototype for rating student performance in traditional institutions. Not every distance education program employs assessment models, however, so individual professors teaching on-line classes will need to rely on available, and sometimes limited, resources for ensuring that students understand assessment expectations.

To help professors use available electronic resources so that students will have clearer knowledge of professorial assessment expectations, I provide suggestions for designing a solid syllabus, using the available technology, and creating a student-centered atmosphere.

Designing a Solid Syllabus

In both the on-line and the traditional class, a syllabus is the foundation for the course and serves as the professor's contract with students. Although syllabi content vary across departments and disciplines, most contain descriptive information such as course title and catalogue description, course goals, reading assignments, writing assignments, schedule, evaluation, and grading practices (Lindemann, 1987). In addressing these components, the syllabus must be thorough and comprehensive enough to give students an overview of the entire curricular scheme, and it should accommodate unexpected turns in the learning process (Schweizer, 1999). For assessment purposes, the syllabus should provide guidelines for grading that are presented to students in an accessible, user-friendly format, such as the format used for grading rubrics.

Grading Rubrics

Norton and Wiburg (1998) define *rubric* as "an established and written set of criteria for scoring student performance on tests, portfolios, writing samples, presentations, products, or other performance tasks" (p. 235). Grading rubrics are a vital part of the grading process in traditional and on-line classrooms because they provide students with written criteria for evaluation at the outset of an assignment and allow students to follow the criteria when planning, drafting, and revising course assignments.

Many professors endorse rubrics as a reliable strategy for assessing student work (Simonson, 2000; Morrison and Ross, 1998). However, they have a tendency to decrease creativity in some students, who turn in "mechanical" assignments (Morrison and Ross, 1998, p. 76). Due to the vast array of possible measuring criteria, rubrics must be carefully devised. Schweizer (1999) advises that rubrics may materialize as anything from "a simple checklist to a detailed analysis" (p. 32).

Exhibit 9.1 is a sample rubric from a twenty-five-point visual design assignment used in a computer-enhanced business communication class. Students were instructed to evaluate an existing document, write an analysis for revision, and redesign the document. Three major categories for evaluation are listed, along with the point values.

Exhibit 9.1. Rubric for Visual Design Assignment

Criterion	Point Value	Questions
(A) Content of analysis paper	10	Are design flaws of the original document specifically designated (named) and described in detail?
		Have at least three basic needs of the target audience been identified and explained?
		Have at least three characteristics of the original purpose for the document been identified and explained?
		Is the rationale for design revisions and changes supported by textual evidence (for example, chapter references, articles)?
(B) Redesign of document	10	Has the document been redesigned to meet the needs of the target audience, which were identified in the analysis?
		Are the main ideas in the redesign consistent with the original purpose, as identified in the analysis?
		Has appropriate use of the following design elements been made (as indicated in the text and other course resources)?
		•White space
		•Bullets
		•Headings
		•Graphics
		•Color
		•Additional design elements
(C) Format and surface errors in A and B	5	Has the information been reorganized so the message is clear (comprehensible) and concise (not wordy) for the target audience?
		Are active verbs used to discuss the revisions?
		Have misspellings and grammatical errors been eliminated?

On-line students will benefit from inclusion of grading rubrics as a link from the syllabus screen on your Web site (Picciano, 2001). If you are unable to provide grading criteria for all assignments on the first day of class, it will be helpful to provide them as early as possible in advance of each assignment and activity.

Using the Technology

Execution of on-line courses is not uniform and differs from institution to institution and professor to professor. In one case, classes may include any combination of synchronous multimedia capabilities, such as videoconferencing. In another, a traditional class may meet in a department's computer lab twice a week to participate in an on-line discussion. A key factor in relaying assessment expectations to students lies in tailoring electronic correspondences to meet the course goals and objectives. This can be achieved by syllabus postings on the Web (or Web postings), Internet features such as scrolling banners, and e-mail messages.

Syllabus Postings. On the first day of class in traditional courses, students typically review print copies of the syllabus. Computer-assisted and computer-enhanced classes may incorporate an uploaded hypertext version of the syllabus on the World Wide Web. If the print document is lost or misplaced, students have a virtual backup copy to rely on. Antonymous to the traditional class, an electronic version of the course goals and requirements is all that is provided in an on-line course. Fortunately, students do tend to print out longer documents that originate on-line (Berge, 2000), especially due to the limitations of the computer screen. As an added benefit, Web syllabi also afford opportunities to revise or update information instantly.

A well-designed syllabus includes relevant target dates, information that students usually need to locate in more than one place. In addition to printing due dates on the syllabus, the on-line teacher can reproduce them as assignment "sheets" on the Internet. Separate links for the assignment sheets or guide sheets for each paper or project make navigation easier for students. Also, placing the due date at the top of the "page" with the title or goal of the class assignment or project makes the information prominent for student recall.

Scrolling Banners. With the endless variations in Web page design, on-line instructors can choose their own navigation or special features to enhance communication with students. The main objective is to generate techniques that are comparable to the traditional class. Further equivalency may be created by "employ[ing] a variety of technologies to help students achieve learning outcomes" (Simonson, 2000, pp. 29–30). Scrolling banners are useful for transmitting reminders on upcoming projects.

Throughout a term, students enrolled in multiple course hours must be reminded of upcoming responsibilities. For example, a composition class may need to be given verbal prompts to begin each phase of a lengthy research paper: finding sources, writing bibliography cards, taking notes, writing the rough draft, and so forth. Engineering students may benefit from cues to begin meeting with a group for a collaborative endeavor. Members of a dance class may need to be reminded to pass out invitations and distribute flyers for a performance. In a traditional classroom, verbal notices can occur anywhere from several weeks to several days in advance (and anytime in between). The same can be true in the on-line class. Professors might incorporate scrolling banners designated for updates or revisions to keep students well informed of course emendations and expectations.

E-Mail Messages. Another factor that may clarify expectations for students in terms of grading is e-mailed instructor comments: "Although e-mail communication does not take the place of personal interaction with your students, it offers instructors the advantage of being able to respond promptly but thoroughly to student questions, perhaps even by including an article or a citation in the reply" (Anderson, Benjamin, Busiel, and Paredes-Holt, 1998, p. 25). On-line professors may be attracted to the idea of providing in-depth comments on assignments by e-mail to counterbalance the lack of face-to-face contact with students. E-mail can also be used to construct a student-centered atmosphere that encourages students to ask for assistance and clarification concerning assessment.

Creating a Student-Centered Atmosphere. Teaching in a computer-mediated environment compromises the nonverbal and verbal cues that are the hallmarks of traditional classrooms: the raised eyebrow, the sweeping hand gestures, vocal intonations. Integrating as many communicative elements into the on-line class as possible can personalize the cyberclassroom. E-mail is a practical conduit for achieving this result.

On-line interpersonal interaction should create a forum that permits individuality to transcend the boundaries of space and time on the computer network. Some tips for achieving stasis include using students' names in your replies and responding to messages within twenty-four hours (Young, 2000). Schweizer (1999) also suggests meeting the psychological needs of students by sending e-mail to quiet or reserved students who would profit from additional support. Adding these and other personal touches to the on-line classroom will help to create an atmosphere in which students feel more comfortable addressing their concerns about the course, including matters of assessment.

Conclusion

The chapter recommendations on preparing students to be assessed in the on-line classroom are by no means exhaustive. Rather, they serve as a starting point for on-line professors with limited expertise or resources. Making traditional classroom strategies work in on-line classrooms is a process of trial and error. In response to comments such as "I don't understand how I got this grade," professors seek whatever effective means will provide an antidotal end to students' assessment sufferings.

References

Anderson, D., Benjamin, B., Busiel, C., and Paredes-Holt, B. *Teaching On-Line: Internet, Research, Conversation and Composition.* White Plains, N.Y.: Longman, 1998.

Berge, Z. L. "Components of the On-Line Classroom." In R. Weiss, D. Knowlton, and B. Speck (eds.), *Principles of Effective Teaching in the On-Line Classroom.* San Francisco: Jossey-Bass, 2000.

Canada, M. "Students as Seekers in On-Line Courses." In R. Weiss, D. Knowlton, and B. Speck (eds.), *Principles of Effective Teaching in the On-Line Classroom.* San Francisco: Jossey-Bass, 2000.

Carnevale, D. "Assessment Takes Center Stage in On-Line Learning: Distance Educators See the Need to Prove That They Teach Effectively." *Chronicle of Higher Education,* 2001. [http://www.chronicle.com/weekly/v47/i31/31a04301.html].

Lindemann, E. *A Rhetoric for Writing Teachers.* New York: Oxford University Press, 1987.

Monaghan, P. "Union Leaders Raise Concerns About Technology for Teaching." *Chronicle of Higher Education,* March 15, 1996, p. A26. [http://www.chronicle.com/che-data/articles.dir/art-42.dir/issue-27.dir/27a02601.html].

Morrison, G., and Ross, S. "Evaluating Technology-Based Processes and Products." In R. Anderson and B. Speck (eds.), *Changing the Way We Grade Student Performance: Classroom Assessment and the New Learning Paradigm.* San Francisco: Jossey-Bass, 1998.

Norton, P., and Wiburg, K. *Teaching with Technology.* Fort Worth, Tex.: Harcourt Brace, 1998.

Picciano, A. *Distance Learning: Making Connections Across Virtual Space and Time.* Upper Saddle River, N.J.: Prentice Hall, 2001.

Schweizer, H. *Designing and Teaching an On-Line Course: Spinning Your Web Classroom.* Needham Heights, Mass.: Allyn and Bacon, 1999.

Simonson, M. "Making Decisions: The Use of Electronic Technology in On-Line Classrooms." In R. Weiss, D. Knowlton, and B. Speck (eds.), *Principles of Effective Teaching in the Online Classroom.* San Francisco: Jossey-Bass, 2000.

Young, J. "Logging in with. . . . Ken W. White: Advice for the On-Line Instructor: Keep It Interpersonal." *Chronicle of Higher Education,* January 28, 2000, p. A44. [http://www.chronicle.com/weekly/v46/i21/21a04401.html]

MICHELE L. FORD is a doctoral student in the rhetoric and professional communication program at Iowa State University, Ames.

10

As on-line degree programs are made available in greater numbers, the necessity of employing clearly articulated criteria for consistent evaluation across programs becomes increasingly evident. The best starting point for such assessment efforts is "Best Practices for Electronically Offered Degree and Certificate Programs," developed by the Western Interstate Commission for Higher Education.

Assessing the On-Line Degree Program

Joe Law, Lory Hawkes, Christina Murphy

The past two decades have witnessed a burgeoning of on-line courses, and many educators have received these developments enthusiastically. For example, Lim (2001) concludes that the movement toward on-line instruction has had significant pedagogical consequences: "The method of delivery shifted from cognitivist-oriented to social-constructivist oriented, and was complemented with a shift in the mode of assessment from summative to more formative evaluation" (p. 19). While many researchers describe similar outcomes for on-line classes and, by extension, entire on-line degree programs, their analyses often call for further investigation and the development of a clearly articulated set of criteria for consistent evaluation across programs (Bryan, 1999; Castro, 1999; Goodwin, 1993; Sullivan, 1999).

The Challenges of Assessing On-Line Programs

The ever-growing range of programs offered and the varied nature of institutional structures set up for their delivery represent both the richness of on-line offerings and the complexities institutions face in assessing quality. This situation is made even more complex by the technological issues that institutions must address in establishing and maintaining their virtual offerings. They must revamp their distributed networks to receive increased traffic while building toward improved bandwidth, retrain their faculty to use Web technologies to organize syllabi and handouts into on-line documents, determine how to protect intellectual property rights in response to the Digital Millennium Copyright Act (1998), and reassess how they accommodate users with disabilities in the light of the W3C Web Accessibility Initiative (World Wide Web Consortium, 2001).

Simply defining the nature of an on-line degree program is itself problematic. Some on-line degree programs are extremely loosely defined, asking students to select courses that will allow them to demonstrate certain competencies in a number of areas. The institution that will award the degree may teach no classes itself but directs students to any number of providers, a term that embraces commercial enterprises as well as more traditional schools, ranging from community colleges to doctorate-granting universities. At the other end of the spectrum is the program created when a single institution makes one or more of its traditional courses of study available on-line. Between those two extremes, the possible variations are limitless. For instance, the degree-granting entity may offer only a portion of its program requirements on-line (perhaps only courses in the major), or it may be a member of a consortium formed to serve the needs of a geographical region or share resources to create a unique program unavailable at any single campus. Understandably, then, the nature of these institutions, their clientele, and the goals of these programs will differ radically, making it impossible to create a single instrument for evaluating all on-line programs.

An important early effort to articulate some common principles for assessment of on-line programs was a three-year project carried out by the Western Cooperative for Educational Telecommunications (Krauth, 1996). This work became the basis of "Best Practices for Electronically Offered Degree and Certificate Programs," developed and published by the Western Interstate Commission for Higher Education (WICHE). The resulting document (2001) has been endorsed by all eight regional accrediting commissions, which have issued a joint statement of commitment to it, calling it "a comprehensive and demanding expression of what is considered current best practice" (Higher Learning Commission, 2000, final paragraph).

In the light of that endorsement, any attempt to develop an assessment plan for on-line programs should begin with WICHE's "Best Practices" document. It lays out these practices in five categories:

- Consistency of program with institutional mission
- Provisions for program oversight and accountability
- Provision of faculty support
- Provision of student support
- Implementation of evaluation and assessment measures

This chapter discusses each of these key areas by outlining in general terms the range of concerns within each category that must be considered in developing assessment measures for specific on-line degree programs within their unique institutional contexts.

Consistency of Program with Institutional Mission

The program should be consistent with the stated role and mission of the institution, and policy statements issued by the institution should reflect its commitment to the students for whom the program was designed. Budgets too should indicate the institution's commitment to the program, supplying resources for adequate technical and physical support. This aspect is especially challenging technically and financially to institutions. Since virtual universities provide instruction and information on demand to enrolled students, they must maintain a twenty-four-hour operation. To keep the educational sites going, some institutions have brought more servers online and, with sophisticated load-balancing techniques, have channeled the overflow of users to secondary servers that contain identical content. These mirror sites also forestall hacker disruptions since a secondary server can quickly be made the primary server.

Bandwidth, the capacity to carry a signal, is rapidly increasing, which escalates the power of distributed university networks. As bandwidth increases, so does the potential for better transmission of more memory-rich media. Obviously, the financial requirements of offering such services represent challenges for the majority of institutions and also determine how they assess their technical capabilities for offering high-quality on-line programs.

Provisions for Program Oversight and Accountability

The institution's internal organizational structure should provide for the oversight of the program, including academic oversight. The technical framework required for the program should be coherent and consistent with that of the larger institution. In addition, the institution must take into account articulation and transfer policies with respect to the program in question. Also, it is crucial that curriculum and pedagogy, rather than concerns for the availability or cost benefits of the technology, drive the program. As with any other academic program, on-line programs of study should lead to "collegiate level learning outcomes appropriate to the rigor and breadth of the degree or certificate awarded by the institution" (Higher Learning Commission, 2000, sec. 2a). Thus, when a degree is to be awarded, the on-line program should be consistent with other courses of study leading to the same degree, including general education requirements.

A related issue stems from the recognition that "traditional faculty roles may be unbundled and/or supplemented" during the development of new on-line programs; thus, the full participation of academically qualified people in all aspects of the program, including oversight, is a major concern (Higher Learning Commission, 2000, sec. 2b). Furthermore, institutions must provide a coherent plan to enable all students "to access all courses necessary to complete the program," especially in programs that mix on-campus elements with electronic ones (sec. 2c).

Another important concern for evaluation (and accountability) arises when an institution relies on outside providers of one kind or another. The eight regional accrediting commissions clearly specify that the responsibility for curriculum and instruction remains with the institution awarding the degree, even when "important elements of a program may be supplied by

consortial partners or outsourced to other organizations, including con-
tractors who may not be accredited" (Higher Learning Commission, 2000,
sec. 2d). This responsibility includes the use of qualified faculty, the management and delivery of suitable course materials, and the availability and
quality of technical services for faculty and students alike. Also, "appropriate interaction (synchronous or asynchronous) between instructor and students and among students" should be reflected in everything involved with
the program (sec. 2e).

Provision of Faculty Support

The third major category is prefaced with the acknowledgment that the
"increasingly diverse and reorganized" faculty roles associated with on-line
programs call for special attention. In some situations, the person who
develops a course might not be the one who instructs students. Such changing conditions make it particularly important to examine how—and how
explicitly—on-line programs deal with such faculty-related issues as deter-
mination of workload and compensation, the way in which working with
on-line programs is factored into professional evaluation, and the much-
contested area of the ownership of intellectual property (Higher Learning
Commission, 2000, sec. 3a). In addition, more straightforward issues of faculty support must be considered, such as the institution's provisions for
ongoing technical, design, and production support (sec. 3b); its provisions
for orientation and training in specific technologies, including upgrades and
other new developments (sec. 3c); and its provisions for training faculty in
"strategies for effective interaction" in working with students (sec. 3d).
Furthermore, institutions must now conform to new guidelines to protect
the intellectual property of their faculty who create on-line courses. Since
1997, the W3C Web Accessibility Initiative has conducted an investigation
and created a three-tier checkpoint guideline for designing Web sites.
Furthermore, the 1998 Digital Millennium Copyright Act specifies that universities must take reasonable measures to prevent access to copyrighted
material. The act outlines the limitations of fair use claims in relation to
electronic files and places liability on institutions to seek copyright com-
pliance in order to protect the intellectual property rights of authors.

Provision of Student Support

Noting the changes in today's students and the growing complexities of
serving them effectively, the "Best Practices" document suggests ways an
on-line program should deal appropriately with students before admitting
them, such as clearly communicating the technical competencies required,
access requirements, the costs of the program and the likely time to com-
pletion, the services available, and the special requirements of independent
learning. Institutions should also ensure that all services (including those

connected with advising, placement, enrollment, financial aid, tutoring, and technology assistance) are made available to students not physically present on campus and should recognize as well the necessity of building some sense of community, such as through study groups, student directories, and invitations to campus events.

Implementation of Evaluation and Assessment Measures

Evaluation and assessment are recognized as a special challenge for on-line programs, and the document calls for "sustained, evidence-based and participatory inquiry" (Higher Learning Commission, 2000, sec. 5) as to whether these programs are achieving their identified learning objectives. Other concerns include systematic safeguards for the integrity of the program, such as establishing "firm student identification" for exams (sec. 5a). Besides investigating the correspondence between student achievement and the program's intended outcomes, other measures suggested are retention rates, student satisfaction surveys, faculty satisfaction surveys, institutional data indicating the extent to which students not previously served are now being served, measures of student competence in "fundamental skills such as communication, comprehension, and analysis" (sec. 5d), and analyses of the cost-effectiveness of program to students.

Conclusion

Undoubtedly, competition from for-profit companies will continue to have a major impact on how institutions will structure and assess on-line degree programs (Young, 2001). For example, the ability to cash in on improved bandwidth for educational delivery has produced new competitors. Large publishing companies (among them, the Pearson Group, Houghton Mifflin, and McGraw-Hill) are turning their textbook archives and their publishing expertise into educational ventures with faculty and a support staff for a cadre of students enrolling in their virtual universities. More than ever before, as institutions are straining to provide reliable, full-time operation of information-intensive sites that are easily scanned and easily navigated, they are also faced with the dilemma of technology transfer. Some institutions solve the problem by dividing the roles of delivery and instruction. They hire media specialists to work with faculty who develop the instructional design. Other institutions adopt course design software like WebCT or Blackboard, which simplify the design of a course Web and reduce decision making to a mouse click selection of options. Other institutions band together in a geographical consortium to further technology training. For example, twenty-three colleges in Maryland have formed the Faculty Online Technology Training Consortium to train faculty to teach in a virtual classroom and to return to their campuses and mentor others.

Certainly, the challenges that institutions face with the demand for and spiraling costs of new technology, increased competition from the for-profit sector, new legal guidelines concerning intellectual property rights, and the complex requirements of hiring, training, and retaining faculty with the technical mastery to provide on-line delivery of degree programs will shape the nature of future on-line programs and also determine the methods by which such programs will be assessed and held accountable. In this regard, the "Best Practices" document provides direction for assessment in stating that all data gathered from the evaluation of on-line programs should serve as part of a larger project of "continual self-evaluation directed toward program improvement" that will guide curriculum design and delivery, pedagogy, and budgeting decisions (Higher Learning Commission, 2000, sec. 5e). Taken as a whole, these data should not only support the mission of the institution but also clarify and perhaps even redefine that mission.

References

Bryan, J. L. "The Identification and Relationship of the Type of Support and Resources Faculty Require to Design, Produce, and Teach On-Line." Unpublished doctoral dissertation, University of Southern California, 1999.

Castro, C. M. de. "An Analysis of the Perceptions of Community College Leaders Regarding Good Practices of Distance Education at New Jersey Community Colleges." Unpublished doctoral dissertation, University of Sarasota, 1999.

Digital Millennium Copyright Act of 1998. Pub. L. No. 105–304, 112 Stat. 2860–2918, 1998.

Goodwin, B. N. "A Study of the Perceptions and Attitudes Exhibited by Distance Education Students and Faculty at the University of Phoenix ONLINE Program." Unpublished doctoral dissertation, Pepperdine University, 1993.

Higher Learning Commission of the North Central Association of Colleges and Schools. "Best Practices for Electronically Offered Degree and Certificate Programs." [http://www.ncahigherlearningcommission.org/resources/electronic_degrees/]. July 22, 2000.

Krauth, B. "Principles of Good Practice for Distance Learning Programs." *Cause/Effect,* 1996, *19*(1), 6–8.

Lim, C. P. "A Holistic Approach Towards the Use of an Integrated On-Line Delivery and Management System." *Journal of Educational Media,* 2001, *26*(1), 19–33.

Sullivan, J. W. "Statewide On-Line Web-Based Training Program to Prepare New Jersey Community College Faculty for Distance Teaching." Unpublished doctoral dissertation, Nova Southeastern University, 1999.

Western Interstate Commission for Higher Education. "Best Practices for Electronically Offered Degree and Certificate Programs." [http://www.wiche.edu/telecom/Accrediting%20-%20Best%20Practices.pdf]. Mar. 13, 2001.

World Wide Web Consortium. "Web Accessibility Initiative (WAI)." [http://www.w3.org/WAI/]. June 28, 2001.

Young, J. R. "Maryland Colleges Train Professors to Teach On-Line." *Chronicle of Higher Education,* Aug. 10, 2001, p. A48.

Joe Law is associate professor of English and coordinator of Writing Across the Curriculum at Wright State University, Dayton, Ohio.

Lory Hawkes is senior professor of general education at DeVry University in Dallas, Texas.

Christina Murphy is dean of the College of Liberal Arts and professor of English at Marshall University in Huntington, West Virginia.

This chapter focuses on the user interface and
instructional design of on-line materials: accessibility,
aesthetic appeal, consistency and layout,
customizability and maintainability, help and support
documentation, intimacy and presence, metaphors and
maps, and other items.

Assessing the Usability of On-Line Instructional Materials

Brad Mehlenbacher

Although cognitive and educational psychologists have studied learning for decades, establishing just how moving conventional instruction on-line improves or detracts from learning continues to be hotly debated. And along with the fundamental challenge of defining learning and how we implement Web-based instruction (WBI), we also need to pay attention to the interface challenges posed by these evolving domains (Rappin, Guzdial, Realff, and Ludovice, 1997).

Research on user-centered design, usability, and human-computer interaction can provide instructors with numerous informal but powerful methods to help them design WBI that is functional and supports the range of activities that users are expected to perform and is aesthetically pleasing and supports user expectations, scanning, search, and reading goals.

A Sociocognitive Model of On-Line Instruction

Before describing methods that can help instructors understand user behavior and design usable WBI, it is important to acknowledge that all instruction, whether on-line or conventional, involves interaction. Moore's notion of transactional distance (1992) is critical to understanding how on-line or distance education interacts with and complements traditional definitions of education, focusing on the amount and types of interaction that occur between learners and instructors and among learners, instructors, and overall WBI design. Education therefore can be viewed as a continuum of transactional offerings, where the specifics of media and mediation are less important than their variety and quality. In this light, it seems more appropriate to frame different educational approaches in terms of whether they are same time–same place instruction or same time–different place instruction.

As unpredictable as learners may be, it is still possible for instructors to develop an instructional plan that anticipates five critical dimensions of all instructional situations: learner background and knowledge, learner tasks, social dynamics, instructional objectives, and learning environment and tools.

Learner Background and Knowledge. Research on hard-copy and on-line documentation suggests that users do not read documentation (Rettig, 1991). This perspective toward users is only partly true: users do not read documentation unless they think they need it (motivation is a critical issue in all learning), and when they do read documentation, they do so strategically: satisficing, skipping, scanning, and skimming.

Human-computer interaction and usability researchers have spent considerable energy trying to anticipate user types, backgrounds, and behaviors. Kearsley (1988), for example, describes three levels or dimensions of user experience: expertise with the computer, the particular task domain, and the particular application software.

Another method of describing learners is in terms of their demographic characteristics, for example, their level of education, economic standing, geographical placement, subcultural values and expectations, or age. This perspective toward users finds its roots ultimately in the North American Industry Classification System (NAICS), produced by the U.S. Department of Commerce, which influences most contemporary marketing analyses of audiences' tastes and preferences.

Learning styles as well influence the way users access information (Kolb, 1984). Felder (1993) suggests that students can be characterized broadly in terms of the type of information they prefer (sights, sounds, or texts), their preferred modality (visual or verbal), their preferred organization of information (inferred or deductive), their approach to processing information (active versus reflective), and how they move toward understanding (sequentially or holistically). Mehlenbacher, Miller, Covington, and Larsen (2000), for example, found that reflective, global learners tended to perform better than hands-on, sequential learners in Web-based courses on communication for engineering and technology.

Finally, it is important to note that learners are subject to a host of particular emotional, motivation, and affective attributes (Mehlenbacher, 2000). User-learners often hold mistaken models of the problems they are working with, and these user misconceptions (Mirel, 1998) can produce "problem tangles" that lead to increasingly confusing mismatches between instruction and user representations of the original problem. These problematic user situations can generate serious errors unless instructors are able to anticipate them in advance to account for them in the WBI.

Learner Tasks and Activities. Users in general move recursively through six goal states as they attempt to work with any on-line environment (Duffy, Palmer, and Mehlenbacher, 1993):

1. Representing problems. Users, guided by prior experience and their ability to apply that experience to their particular situations, attempt to understand their situation or problem as they work through it.
2. Accessing information. Users identify instructional materials relevant to their problem representation and attempt to access them.
3. Navigating information. Users navigate to particular topics, a considerable challenge for many on-line learners.
4. Scanning information. Users search for particular headings, information items, or instructions related to their problem representation.
5. Understanding information. Users attempt to comprehend the instructional text and graphics, a process that is easier to summarize than to produce (Barker, 1998; Schriver, 1997).
6. Transferring information. Users take what they have learned back to the class assignments, discussion, and exercises.

Importantly, these six goals of the general learner orientation, "How do I . . . . ?" are usually framed by cognitive dissonance: "What is due next? Where are the examples of this exercise? What do I need to read to prepare for the next assignment?" and so on.

Social Dynamics. Stelzer and Vogelzangs (1995) stress that the greatest challenge facing on-line instructors is how to generate a high level of student-faculty interaction, given that the greatest difficulty that on-line students experience is feeling isolated and keeping their motivation high. For this reason, carefully anticipating how Web pages, bulletin boards, chat environments, whiteboards, commenting and annotation tools, and e-mail or listservs will work together can allow instructors to anticipate some of the general problems their on-line students are likely to encounter. Limiting the number of tools that instructors integrate into their WBI is one way of decreasing up front the user problems that can occur.

Instructional Objectives. Savery and Duffy (1995) define problem-based learning (PBL) as learner understanding based on experiences with content, context, and the learner's goals, where meaning is not transmitted but contextualized, puzzlement motivates learning, and social negotiation and trial and error are important aspects of all learning situations.

Instructors should therefore operate as coaches or facilitators, an orientation that for many requires a significant reorientation. Rather than focusing on the one-way communication of course content, instructors need to communicate instructional objects though discussion, elaboration, confirmation, sharing, questioning, introducing, and adapting. As much as possible, on-line students need to be able to take an active role in the learning process, not only for motivational reasons but also for practical ones:

instructors cannot possibly hope to keep up with the incoming requests for their direction if their students default to them as the single authority for the class content.

Learning Environment and Tools. Moore (1992) suggests that as more instructors move their classrooms on-line, another type of interaction will become increasingly important: student-environment interaction (see Khan, 1997, for numerous chapters that focus specifically on this dimension). The environment in general refers to the physical or Web-based location for learning, which may include specific on-line tools that students interact with, such as e-mail, listserv programs, MOOs (multi-user domains, object-oriented), chatrooms, network file exchange platforms, forums, and computer-conferencing software (Eldred and Hawisher, 1995). Environments may be well designed and easy to navigate, convenient, reliable, accurate, and comprehensive, or they may be the opposite.

Usability Testing WBI

Instructors and information developers interested in learning more about usability testing should acquaint themselves with the numerous resources available on the subject (Alder and Winograd, 1992; Dumas and Redish, 1993; Hackos and Redish, 1998; Nielsen, 1997; Nielsen and Mack, 1994; Rubin, 1994).

Many different approaches to usability testing exist, ranging from contextual inquiry to interviews and surveying to focus groups and market analyses to direct user observation.[1] Importantly, every method has its strengths and weaknesses, and readers interested in learning more about the details of usability approaches should consult Mehlenbacher (1993).

For the purposes of this chapter, I recommend that observation-based usability testing combined with the talk-aloud protocol method is probably the least expensive and most rewarding data-collection approach for instructors to take. To run an observation-based usability test and talk-aloud protocol, instructors simply ask users (representative of their intended audience) to perform four or five tasks with the WBI while talking aloud. The usual test duration is thirty minutes to one hour and includes having users sign consent forms that allow the instructor to analyze the data collected from their audiotaped or videotaped session, demographic information surveys, and posttest questionnaires that focus on quantitative reactions to the WBI.

Heuristic Evaluation of WBI

Mack and Nielsen (1994) warn that "usability inspection methods are well suited as part of an iterative design process where they can be combined with other usability evaluation methods like user testing" (p. 19). Heuristic procedures, unlike rule-governed procedures, gain their strength from their flexibility, allowance for intuition and judgment, and general goal of problem solving (see Table 11.1 for an extensive list of heuristic questions for evaluators to consider as they design WBI).

Table 11.1. Usability Design Principles for WBI

Usability Design Principles for Web-Based Instruction (WBI), 1 of 2 (cf. Najjar, 1998; Nielsen, 1994; Selber, Johnson-Eilola, and Mehlenbacher, 1997)

Accessibility	Has the WBI been viewed on different platforms, browsers, modem speeds? Is the WBI ADA compliant (e.g., have you avoided the use of colors such as red and yellow which are problematic for visually challenged users)? Have you consulted the Center for Applied Special Technology's Bobby (http://www.cast.org/bobby) or W3C's Web Assessibility Initiative (http://www.w3.org/WAI)?
Aesthetic appeal	Does the design appear minimalist (uncluttered, readable, memorable)? Are graphics or colors employed aesthetically? Are distractions minimized (e.g., movement, blinking, scrolling, animation, etc.)?
Authority and authenticity	Does the WBI establish a serious tone or presence? Are humor or anthropomorphic expressions used minimally? Is direction given for further assistance if necessary?
Completeness	Are levels clear and explicit about the "end" or parameters of the Web-based course? Are there different "levels" of use and, if so, are they clearly distinguishable?
Consistency and layout	Does every page begin with a title/subject heading that describes the contents? Is there a consistent icon design and graphic display across pages or screens? Are the layout, font choices, terminology use, colors, and positioning of items the same throughout the WBI (<4 of any of the above is usually recommended)?
Customizability and maintainability	Does printing of the WBI require special configuration to optimize presentation and, if so, is this indicated in the documentation? Are individual preferences/sections clearly distinguishable from one another? Is manipulation of the WBI possible and easy to achieve?
Error support and feedback	When users scan or select something does it differentiate itself from other information chunks or unselected items? Do cross-references, menu instructions, prompts, and error messages (if necessary) appear in the same place on each page or screen?
Examples and case studies	Are examples, demonstrations, case studies, or problem-based situations available to facilitate learning? Are examples divided into meaningful sections (e.g., overview, demonstration, explanation, and so on)?
Genre representation	Is task-oriented help or support materials easy to locate and access? Is the WBI's "table of contents" or main menu organized functionally, according to user tasks and not according to instructional jargon or generic "topics"?

Table 11.1. (Continued)

Usability Design Principles for Web-Based Instruction (WBI), 2 of 2

Intimacy and presence	Is an overall tone of the WBI present, active, and engaging? Does the WBI act as a learning environment for users, and not simply as a warehouse of unrelated topics or links?
Metaphors and maps	Does the WBI establish an easily recognizable metaphor that helps users identify additional instructional materials in relation to each other, their state in the system, and options available to them?
Navigability and user movement	Does the WBI clearly separate navigation from content? How many levels down can users traverse and, if more than three, is returning to their initial state easy to accomplish? Can users see where they are in the overall WBI at all times? Do the locations of navigational elements remain consistent (e.g., tabs or menus)? Is the need to scroll or traverse multiple pages for a single topic minimized across screens or pages?
Organization and information relevance	Is a site map or comprehensive index available? Is the overall organization of the WBI clear from the majority of pages or screens? Are primary options emphasized in favor of secondary and tertiary ones?
Readability and quality of writing	Is the text in active voice and concisely written (>4 <15 words/sentence)? Are terms consistently plural, verb + object or noun + verb, avoiding unnecessarily redundant words? Does white space highlight a modular text design that separates information chunks from each other? Are bold and color texts used sparingly to identify important text (limiting use of all capitals and italics to improve readability)? Can users understand the content of the information presented easily?
Relationship with real-world tasks	Are terminology and labeling meaningful, concrete, and familiar to the target audience? Do related and interdependent WBI functions appear on the same screen or page? Is sequencing used naturally, if sequences of common events are expected? Does the WBI allow users to easily complete their transactions or tasks on-line?
Reliability and functionality	Do all the titles, menus, icons, links, and opening windows work predictably across the WBI?
Typographic cues and structuring	Does the text employ meaningful discourse cues, modularization, chunking? Is information structured by meaningful labeling, bulleted lists, or iconic markers? Are legible fonts and colors employed? Is the principle of left-to-right placement linked to most-important to least-important information?

Conclusion

On-line learning environments are still very much in their infancy, and despite enthusiastic claims that such teaching and learning environments readily exist, instructors and students are still faced with a significant learning curve. Integrating usability testing approaches into the design process can help instructors anticipate some of the problems their students are bound to encounter in providing on-line learning materials that are engaging, memorable, and easy to read and use.

Note

1. See Horn, "The Usability Methods Toolbox," http://jthom.best.vwh.net/usability/usable.htm; Instone, "Usable Web," http://usableWeb.com; and Nielsen, "Usable Information Technology," http://www.useit.com.

References

Alder, P. S., and Winograd, T. A. (eds.). *Usability: Turning Technologies into Tools.* New York: Oxford University Press, 1992.

Duffy, T. M., Palmer, J. E., and Mehlenbacher, B. *On-line Help: Design and Evaluation.* Norwood, N.J.: Ablex, 1993.

Dumas, J. S., and Redish, J. C. *A Practical Guide to Usability Testing.* Norwood, N.J.: Ablex, 1993.

Eldred, J. C., and Hawisher, G. E. "Researching Electronic Networks." *Written Communication,* 1995, *12*(3), 330–359.

Felder, R. M. "Reaching the Second Tier: Learning and Teaching Styles in College Science Education." *Journal of College Science Teaching,* 1993, *23*(5), 286–290.

Hackos, J. T., and Redish, J. C. (1998). *User and Task Analysis for Interface Design.* New York: Wiley, 1998.

Kearsley, G. *On-line Help Systems: Design and Implementation.* Norwood, N.J.: Ablex, 1988.

Khan, B. H. (ed.). *Web-Based Instruction.* Englewood Cliffs, N.J.: Educational Technology Publications, 1997.

Kolb, D. A. *Experiential Learning: Experience as the Source of Learning and Development.* Upper Saddle River, N.J.: Prentice Hall, 1984.

Mack, R. L., and Nielsen, J. "Executive Summary." In J. Nielsen and R. L. Mack (eds.), *Usability Inspection Methods.* New York: Wiley, 1994.

Mehlenbacher, B. "Software Usability: Choosing Appropriate Methods for Evaluating Online Systems and Documentation." In *SIGDOC'93: The Eleventh Annual International Conference Proceedings.* New York: ACM, 1993. [http://www4.ncsu.edu/~brad_m/publications.html].

Mehlenbacher, B. "Intentionality and Other 'Nonsignificant' Issues in Learning: Commentary on Margaret Martinez's 'Intentional Learning in an Intentional World.'" *ACM Journal of Computer Documentation,* 2000, *24*(1), 25–30.

Mehlenbacher, B., Miller, C. R., Covington, D., and Larsen, J. "Active and Interactive Learning Online: A Comparison of Web-Based and Conventional Writing Classes." *IEEE Transactions on Professional Communication,* 2000, *43*(2), 166–184.

Mirel, B. "Minimalism for Complex Tasks." In J. M. Carroll (ed.), *Minimalism Beyond the Nurnberg Funnel.* Cambridge, Mass.: MIT Press, 1998.

Moore, M. G. "Distance Education Theory." *American Journal of Distance Education,* 1992, *5*(3), 1–6.

Najjar, L. J. "Principles of Educational Multimedia User Interface Design." *Human Factors,* 1998, *40*(2), 311–323.

Nielsen, J. "Heuristic Evaluation." In J. Nielsen and R. L. Mack (eds.), *Usability Inspection Methods.* New York: Wiley, 1994.

Nielsen, J. "Usability Engineering." In A. B. Tucker, Jr. (ed.), *The Computer Science and Engineering Handbook.* Boca Raton, Fla.: CRC Press, 1997.

Nielsen, J., and Mack, R. L. (eds.). *Usability Inspection Methods.* New York: Wiley, 1994.

Rappin, N., Guzdial, M., Realff, M., and Ludovice, P. "Balancing Usability and Learning in an Interface." *Proceedings of ACM CHI 97 Conference on Human Factors in Computing Systems,* 1997, *1,* 479–486.

Rettig, M. "Nobody Reads Documentation." *Communications of the ACM,* 1991, *34*(7), 19–24.

Rubin, J. *Handbook of Usability Testing: How to Plan, Design, and Conduct Effective Tests.* New York: Wiley, 1994.

Savery, J. R., and Duffy, T. M. "Problem Based Learning: An Instructional Model and Its Constructivist Framework." *Educational Technology,* 1995, *35*(5), 31–38.

Selber, S. A., Johnson-Eilola, J. D., and Mehlenbacher, B. "Online Support Systems: Tutorials, Documentation, and Help." In A. B. Tucker, Jr. (ed.), *The Computer Science and Engineering Handbook.* Boca Raton, Fla.: CRC Press, 1997.

Stelzer, M., and Vogelzangs, I. "Isolation and Motivation in Online and Distance Learning Courses." [http://www.to.utwente.nl/ism/On-line95/Campus/library/on-line94/chap8/chap8.htm]. 1995.

U.S. Department of Commerce, National Technical Information Service. *North American Industry Classification System.* Springfield, Va.: U.S. Department of Commerce, 1997. [http:www.ntis.gov/product/naics.htm]

BRAD MEHLENBACHER *is an associate professor in technical communication (English) and an adjunct faculty member in ergonomics and experimental psychology at North Carolina State University. He also serves as usability consultant for the new North Carolina State University Web site.*

12

The effectiveness of on-line assessment is challenged by several significant factors: unrealistic appraisal of the potential of on-line education, enforcement of a code of conduct, and computer and telecommunication skills bias and other limitations of on-line media.

Epilogue: A Cautionary Note About On-Line Assessment

Richard Thomas Bothel

One of the most significant challenges in on-line course delivery is the testing and assessment component (Finkelstein and others, 2000). On-line education provides an important tool to help shape the future of education, but the effectiveness of assessment is challenged by three factors reviewed in this chapter: unrealistic appraisal of the potential of on-line education, enforcement of a code of conduct, and computer and telecommunication skills bias and other limitations of the on-line media.

Unrealistic Appraisal of the Potential of On-Line Education

The future of on-line instruction is threatened by the unrealistic appraisal of its potential. Technologies today make it possible to deliver any course on-line enhanced with advanced media. However, the largest threat to the assessment of on-line activities or any other aspect of the on-line educational process is trying to deliver every class on-line. Although we live in an "anything's possible with technology" world, it does not mean that on-line education provides the most effective or even the most efficient delivery methodology for every class. Assessment of on-line courses cannot be effective or efficient if a course is placed on-line that is not appropriate for this medium.

On-line education is caught up in the general tumult surrounding the use of technology in higher education. Since the introduction of the microcomputer in the 1980s, technology has been developed on campuses in a piecemeal and unsystematic manner. Educational goals have been second-ary to organizational or financial considerations (Katz, 2001). Although advocates of on-line education often cite studies such as Russell's well-known "No Significant Difference Phenomenon" (1999) as proof of the util-itarianism of distance education, there have not been major and universally accepted assessments of on-line learning that permit objective opinions to be formed. Although on-line educators may be taking a leadership role in talking about student outcome assessment, not many distance education programs rely on assessment models (Carneval, 2001). Furthermore, it is the weakness of research on the effect of the traditional classroom environ-ment that makes it difficult to draw specific conclusions regarding assess-ment of on-line activities.

On-line education continues to proliferate without adequate assess-ment of its outcomes. Even more dangerous, top-level administrators do not rely on even limited assessment results to make decisions on the expan-sion of on-line programs. Too often, administrators have used technology on their campuses evidenced by on-line programs as a mantle of educa-tional innovation showing parents, governing boards, and legislators how superb their campuses are with fiber-optics and advanced media centers.

On-line education is found on campuses serving resident students who may be better served in the classroom or with some form of Web-enhanced class. There is considerable confusion as to what objective providing on-line courses really is trying to achieve. The use of a tool has been confused for a goal (O'Donnel, 1998). It is a dangerous assumption that on-line courses can be used across all types and sizes of institutions (Hawkins, 1999). It should be remembered that there still exist the traditional teaching meth-ods that have been handed down from ancient philosophers to the little red schoolhouses (Maier, 2001). The traditional classroom continues to be best for many students, and they cannot be fairly assessed in the on-line envi-ronment that may seem foreign to them.

Enforcement of a Code of Conduct

A student code of conduct in the classroom is becoming a major issue in edu-cation, and it is magnified in the on-line classroom. Assessment can be effec-tive only if the vagaries of on-line classes are considered. Eighty percent of high school honors students admit to cheating (Kuperberg, 2000). And the students moving into their college years have no better record. The 1998 Report Card on the Ethics of American Youth (Josephson Institute of Ethics, 1998) indicates that 70 percent of high schoolers admit to cheating on exams.

No matter how effectively the outcomes of a student's work are mea-sured, this assessment has no value if the student who is being assessed is not the same person who is on the class roster. On-line class work provides a broader range of opportunities to conceal true identity and make cheat-ing possible. A number of technology companies are scrambling to provide solutions, but there is little agreement among accreditation bodies as to what an adequate solution to this problem really is. When a professor's only contact with a student is on-line, at some time in the course, the professor still needs some physical verification that the student is truly the student and not a surrogate. When students are able to work in their homes, office, or anywhere else they have access to a computer and the Internet, anyone can log in with the student's ID and complete assignments. Spouses, secretaries, and a variety of other student friends are possible candidates to complete on-line assignments for the student.

Beyond verifying student identity in an on-line course, another challenge to the assessment of on-line student work is plagiarism encouraged by a staggering volume of on-line cheat material (Rooks, 1998). There are thousands of venues available to cheating students (Rice, 2000). For people who are inclined to cheat, it is easier to do so in the on-line situation (Young, 2001). Cheater.com, Cheathouse.com, SchoolSucks.com, SchoolPaper.com, EssayCrawler.com, and NetEssays are just a few of the Internet sites that students can use to cheat.

It may also be that the easy cut-and-paste access to information as the computer access to information expands has blurred for students the meaning of stealing another's work. Students may not even understand what plagiarism is (Roach, 2001). Complicating the situation, Don McCabe, founder of Duke University's Center for Academic Integrity, says it starts with high school teachers' being clueless about the Internet. Students can copy sentences, paragraphs, or full papers with a very low probability of getting caught (Thomas, 2001).

Assessment cannot have meaning unless additional safeguards are included in the on-line course that discourages the Internet cut-and-paste mentality of many students. In addition, assessment of student work must include a verification of student identity.

Computer and Telecommunication Skills Bias and Other Limitations of the On-Line Media

Computer and telecommunication skills and experience can make a great deal of difference in the student's learning experience and success in an on-line course. But how many on-line courses provide the instructor with a postassessment of a student's computer and on-line skills or experience in taking an on-line class?

Face-to-face interaction and social bonds are crucial in education (Shoemaker, 2000). Yet how is human interaction facilitated in the digital environment? Many faculty are anxious about the dehumanization and alienation their students might face in a computer-dominated learning environment (Novek, 1999).

Consistently good on-line student interaction is much more dependent on teacher-facilitator skills than in the traditional classroom. The teacher might have to filter, facilitate, edit, help, or promote what is going on in the on-line class. The on-line teacher must wear many hats and assume technical, managerial, pedagogical, and social roles. Some on-line instructors may have these skills. It is the exception rather than the rule for higher education faculty to be trained in all of these areas. Higher education faculty are conscientious teachers, but the majority have no formal training in teaching and learning alternatives to the traditional classroom environment (Gilbert, 2000). Without this training, it is difficult to have effective student interaction (Bonk, 2000). And how can a student's performance be fairly assessed when it is so closely dependent on teacher skills?

Second, electronic communication cannot completely replace face-to-face communication and other interaction that is needed in some educational activities. Virtual relationships are like having a battery that runs down if it is not recharged periodically by being plugged into real people (Kanter, 2001). How can a professor assess a student's ability to deal with clients in a one-to-one office counseling situation with on-line interaction or assess effective use of body language in the student's electronic communication?

Computer skills are one of the largest barriers to on-line learning (Thiele, Allen, and Stuckey, 1999). Learner computer phobia may even make students refuse to use on-line resources (ASTER, 2001). Students' computer literacy should be assessed prior to the beginning of course work (Carr, 2000). Unfortunately, few programs provide this type of computer skills evaluation in courses outside a specific computer curriculum. The on-line chatroom provides one of the most obvious examples of the problem that even the lack of keyboard skills creates. Sitting in front of a computer and watching chatroom members fly comments back and forth across the screen can be intimidating for computer users with moderate typing skills. The use of the chatroom requires not only good keyboard skills but also the ability to relate to the electronic environment.

A great deal of progress has been made in the standardization and access students have to computers, software, and telecommunications. It is possible to provide on-line programs throughout the world and be assured that students will have access to the Internet and at least a standard browser that enables them to access basic course materials. Unfortunately, there is still a tendency of course developers to attempt to include "bells and whistles" that go beyond the reliable basic hardware and software capabilities on the Internet. The claim is that these technologies are needed to hold a student's attention, but no one considers that they may be unreliable for student use. Studies such as those of Elizabeth Pilcher (2001) at the University of Southern California College of Dental Medicine still continue to show that simple access to course materials through an intranet system, on-line quizzes, and difficulty in printing Web-based materials are problems.

Conclusion

A lesson can be learned from the 1930s with the introduction of the radio or from the 1950s with the advent of the television. Many educators thought that both technologies offered either great opportunities or threats to our democratic society. Some saw the potential of technology to democratize education, while others saw technologies as becoming the tools of fascist leaders to dominate people's thinking (Gilbert, 2001). In spite of these potentials, few changes have been seen in the options faculty provide in their classrooms.

On-line classes and the incorporation of these capabilities in the classroom provide some of the most exciting educational opportunities, but they are not the answer to every educational issue. Many of the problems of simply using traditional assessment methods on on-line courses can be overcome if on-line courses use assessment models that take into account the uniqueness of the on-line environment.

The concept of authentic assessment is not new, but it may answer some of the weaknesses of traditional assessment of on-line course work. Authentic assessment seeks to situate problems and tasks in real-world contexts. It may take the form of paper-and-pencil tasks, performances, and portfolios. What makes this assessment authentic is the extent to which it provides students the opportunity to use their knowledge and skills in accomplishing tasks that they might encounter outside the classroom (Posner and Rudnitsky, 1997). Many institutions specializing in the delivery of on-line courses are already taking the lead in using authentic forms of assessment.

Assessment by itself is not the entire solution. Educators must take a stand against the mass introduction of on-line courses without clearly defined academic objectives. If they do not, any efforts toward effective assessment of students' performance in on-line programs will be lost or clouded by the inappropriate introduction of on-line classes.

References

ASTER (Assisting Small-Group Teaching Through Electronic Resources). "Enhancing Group-Based Learning." Workshop at ILT Annual Conference at the University of York, York, England, July 5, 2001. [http://ctiwebct.york.ac.uk/aster/alt-c_workshop_slides/index.htm].

Bonk, C. "My Hat's on to the On-Line Instructor." *E-Education Advisor*, 2000, *1*(1), 10–14.

Carnevale, D. "Assessment Takes Center Stage in On-Line Learning." *Chronicle of Higher Education*, April 13, 2001, p. A43.

Carr, S. "As Distance Education Comes of Age, the Challenge Is Keeping the Students." *Chronicle of Higher Education*, Feb. 11 2000, p. A39.

Finkelstein, M., Frances, C., Jewett, F., and Scholz, B. *The New Economics of College Teaching and Learning*. Phoenix, Ariz.: American Council on Education/Oryx Press, 2000.

Gilbert, S. "A Widening Gap: The Support Service Crisis." *Syllabus*, 2000, *14*(1), 18, 57.

Gilbert, S. "Dimensions of Technology Change." *Syllabus*, 2001, *14*(12), 28.

Hawkins, B. "Distributed Learning and Institutional Restructuring." *Educom Review*, 1999, *34*(4), 12.

Josephson Institute of Ethics. *1998 Report Card on the Ethics of American Youth*. Marina del Rey, Calif.: Josephson Institute of Ethics, Oct. 19, 1998.

Kanter, R. *Evolve! Succeeding in the Digital Culture of Tomorrow*. Boston: Harvard Business School Press, 2001.

Katz, S. "In Information Technology, Don't Mistake a Tool for a Goal." *Chronicle of Higher Education,* June 15, 2001, pp. 7–9.

Kuperberg, A. "Honestly, Is It Okay to Cheat?" *Behavior Health Digest,* 2000, 2(4), 1.

Maier, T. "Distance Education and the Little Red Cyberschoolhouse." *Community College Week,* 2001, *13*(21), 4.

Novek, E. "Do Professors Dream of Electronic Students? Faculty Anxiety and the New Information Technologies." Paper presented at the Eastern Communication Association Annual Meeting, Charleston, W.Va., May 1999.

O'Donnel, J. *Avatars of the Word: From Papyrus to Cyberspace.* Cambridge, Mass.: Harvard University Press, 1998.

Pilcher, E. "Students' Evaluation of On-Line Materials in Fixed Prosthodontics: A Case Study." *European Journal of Dental Education,* 2001, *5*(2), 53–59.

Posner, G., and Rudnitsky, A. *Course Design: A Guide to Curriculum Development for Teachers.* White Plains, N.Y.: Longman, 1997.

Rice, R. "Plagiarism: The New On-Line Plague." *EduQuery Column.* [http://www.edu query.com/news/plagiarism_on-line_plague.htm]. Jan. 18, 2000.

Roach, R. "Safeguarding Against On-Line Cheating." *Black Issues in Higher Education,* 2001, *18*(8), 92.

Rooks, C. Browsing the Problem. Paper presented at Third Annual Teaching in the Community Colleges On-Line Conference, April 1998, Honolulu, HI.

Russell, T. *No Significant Difference Phenomenon.* Raleigh, N.C.: North Carolina State University, 1999.

Shoemaker, S., Haythornthwaite, C., Kazmer, M., and Robbins, J. "Community Development Among Distance Learners: Temporal and Technological Dimensions." *Journal of Computer-Mediated Communication,* 6(1). [http://www.ascusc.org/ jcmc/vol6/issue1].

Thiele, J., Allen, C., and Stucky, M. "Effects of Web-Based Instruction on Learning Behaviors of Undergraduate and Graduate Students." *Nursing and Health Care Perspectives,* 1999, *20*(4), 199–203.

Thomas, K. "More Students Turn to Virtual Cheating." *Detroit News,* March 22, 2001. [http://detnews.com/2001/technews/0103.23/e03–202306.htm].

Young, J. "A Learning-Technologies Professor Warns That Cheating Is Too Easy: Logging in with M. O. Thirunarayanan." *Chronicle of Higher Education,* Aug. 1, 2000. [http://chronicle.com/free/200108010lu.htm].

RICHARD THOMAS BOTHEL is associate provost for outreach, continuing education, and distance learning at the University of North Carolina–Pembroke.

INDEX

ADA (Americans with Disabilities Act), 62

Alder, P. S., 94

Alternative assessment paradigm: applied to on-line classroom, 14–15; described, 11–12

Anderson, D., 81

Anderson, R. S., 2, 3, 10, 31, 53, 60

Anderson-Inman, L., 41

Aragon, S. R., 61

Assessment: to aid student learning, 24–25; Alternative approach to, 11–12, 14–15; authentic, 10, 103; using bulletin boards for student, 34–35e; using the chatroom for student, 32–34e; competing paradigms of learning-teaching and, 10–12; criticism of focus on surface learning, 10; to evaluate courses, 27–28; five principles applied to group, 46–51; used to monitor student progress, 21–28; "norm referencing," 11; of the on-line degree program, 83–88; on-line field experience, 54, 57–59; paradigm needed for writing, 8–10; preparing for on-line class, 78–81; of student e-folios, 73–75; Traditional paradigm of, 12–14; WBI (Web-based instruction) issues of, 19–20; writing used for learning, 9. *See also* Evaluation; On-line courses

ASTER (Assisting Small-Group Teaching Through Electronic Resources), 102

ATA (Assistive Technology Act of 1998), 62

Atwater, L., 44

Aurbach's Grady Profile, 70

Authentic assessment, 10, 103

Bartlett, K. R., 61

Bauer, J. F., 1, 2, 3, 31, 36

Bean, J. C., 33

Beidler, P. G., 6

Belanoff, P., 69

Benjamin, B., 81

Berge, Z. L., 80

Berzsenyi, C. A., 32

"Best Practices for Electronically Offered Degree and Certificate Programs" (WICHE), 84

Biggs, J., 10

Blackboard's CourseInfo, 20, 38, 54

Blanchard, D., 61, 66

Bok, D., 6, 7

Bonk, C., 102

Bothel, R., 2, 99, 104

Branzburg, J., 20, 27

Breland, H. M., 12

Brown, J. M., 2, 61, 68

Bryan, J. L., 83

Bulletin boards: assessment using, 34–35e; synchronous communication using, 25, 26–27; terms associated with, 32e

Busiel, C., 81

Canada, M., 2, 69, 75, 77

Carey, L., 25

Carnevale, D., 5, 77, 100

Carr, S., 102

Carrotte, P., 6

Case, K. I., 53

Castro, C. M. de, 83

CD-ROM e-folios, 70, 71

Center for Academic Integrity (Duke University), 101

Chatroom: assessment through the, 32–34e; computer skills required for, 102; synchronous communication using, 25, 26, 27; terms associated with, 32e

Cheater.com, 101

Cheathouse.com, 38, 101

Cheating: code of conduct enforcement and, 100–101; on-line course exam, 22; on written projects, 23–24, 38–39, 48, 100–101. *See also* Plagiarizing papers

Chmielewski, C. M., 5

Clinical Experience Rubric, 55e

Code of conduct enforcement, 100–101

Cohen, L., 61, 66

Communication: clarifying grading expectations, 80–81; to create

Back Issue/Subscription Order Form

Copy or detach and send to:

Jossey-Bass, A Wiley Company, 989 Market Street, San Francisco CA 94103-1741

Call or fax toll-free: Phone 888-378-2537 6AM-5PM PST; Fax 888-481-2665

Back issues: Please send me the following issues at $27 each
(Important: please include series initials and issue number, such as TL85)

1. TL _____

_____

_____

$ _____Total for single issues

$ _____ SHIPPING CHARGES: SURFACE

	Domestic	Canadian
First Item	$5.00	$6.00
Each Add'l Item	$3.00	$1.50

For next-day and second-day delivery rates, call the number listed above.

Subscriptions   Please ❑ start ❑ renew my subscription to *New Directions for Teaching and Learning* for the year 2____ at the following rate:

U.S.	❑ Individual $65	❑ Institutional $130
Canada	❑ Individual $65	❑ Institutional $170
All Others	❑ Individual $89	❑ Institutional $204

$ _____Total single issues and subscriptions (Add appropriate sales tax for your state for single issue orders. No sales tax for U.S. subscriptions. Canadian residents, add GST for subscriptions and single issues.)

Federal Tax ID 135593032   GST 89102 8052

❑ Payment enclosed (U.S. check or money order only)

❑ VISA, MC, AmEx, Discover Card # _____ Exp. date_____

Signature _____ Day phone _____

❑ Bill me (U.S. institutional orders only. Purchase order required)

Purchase order #_____

Name _____

Address _____

_____

Phone_____ E-mail _____

For more information about Jossey-Bass, visit our Web site at: www.josseybass.com

PROMOTION CODE = ND3

scholarship of teaching, defines its characteristics and outcomes, and explores its most pressing issues.
ISBN: 0-7879-5447-0

TL85   **Beyond Teaching to Mentoring**
        Alice G. Reinarz, Eric R. White
        Offers guidelines to optimizing student learning through classroom activities as well as peer, faculty, and professional mentoring. Addresses mentoring techniques in technical training, undergraduate business, science, and liberal arts studies, health professions, international study, and interdisciplinary work.
        ISBN: 0-7879-5617-1

TL84   **Principles of Effective Teaching in the Online Classroom**
        Renée E. Weiss, Dave S. Knowlton, Bruce W. Speck
        Discusses structuring the online course, utilizing resources from the World Wide Web and using other electronic tools and technology to enhance classroom efficiency. Addresses challenges unique to the online classroom community, including successful communication strategies, performance evaluation, academic integrity, and accessibility for disabled students.
        ISBN: 0-7879-5615-5

TL83   **Evaluating Teaching in Higher Education: A Vision for the Future**
        Katherine E. Ryan
        Analyzes the strengths and weaknesses of current approaches to evaluating teaching and recommends practical strategies for improving current evaluation methods and developing new ones. Provides an overview of new techniques such as peer evaluations, portfolios, and student ratings of instructors and technologies.
        ISBN: 0-7879-5448-9

TL82   **Teaching to Promote Intellectual and Personal Maturity: Incorporating Students' Worldviews and Identities into the Learning Process**
        Marcia B. Baxter Magolda
        Explores cognitive and emotional dimensions that influence how individuals learn, and describes teaching practices for building on these to help students develop intellectually and personally. Examines how students' unique understanding of their individual experience, themselves, and the ways knowledge is constructed can mediate learning.
        ISBN: 0-7879-5446-2

TL81   **Strategies for Energizing Large Classes: From Small Groups to Learning Communities**
        Jean MacGregor, James L. Cooper, Karl A. Smith, Pamela Robinson
        Describes a comprehensive range of ideas and techniques from informal turn-to-your-neighbor discussions that punctuate a lecture to more complex small-group activities, as well as ambitious curricular reform through learning-community structures.
        ISBN: 0-7879-5337-7

TL80   **Teaching and Learning on the Edge of the Millennium: Building on What We Have Learned**
        Marilla D. Svinicki

Reviews the past and current research on teaching, learning, and motivation. Chapters revisit the best-selling *NDTL* issues, exploring the latest developments in group-based learning, effective communication, teaching for critical thinking, the seven principles for good practice in undergraduate education, teaching for diversity, and teaching in the information age.
ISBN: 0-7879-4874-8

TL79 **Using Consultants to Improve Teaching**
Christopher Knapper, Sergio Piccinin
Provides advice on how to use consultation to improve teaching, giving detailed descriptions of a variety of effective approaches, including classroom observation, student focus groups, small-group instructional diagnosis, faculty learning communities, and action learning.
ISBN: 0-7879-4876-4

TL78 **Motivation from Within: Approaches for Encouraging Faculty and Students to Excel**
Michael Theall
Examines how students' cultural backgrounds and beliefs about knowledge affect their motivation to learn, and applies the latest motivational theory to the instructional process and the university community.
ISBN: 0-7879-4875-6

TL77 **Promoting Civility: A Teaching Challenge**
Steven M. Richardson
Offers strategies for promoting civil discourse and resolving conflict when it arises—both in the classroom and in the campus community at large. Recommends effective responses to disruptive classroom behavior and techniques for encouraging open, respectful discussion of sensitive topics.
ISBN: 0-7879-4277-4

TL76 **The Impact of Technology on Faculty Development, Life, and Work**
Kay Herr Gillespie
Describes ways to enhance faculty members' technological literacy, suggests an approach to instructional design that incorporates the possibilities of today's technologies, and examines how the online community offers an expansion of professional relationships and activities.
ISBN: 0-7879-4280-4

TL75 **Classroom Assessment and Research: An Update on Uses, Approaches, and Research Findings**
Thomas Angelo
Illustrates how classroom assessment techniques (CATs) enhance both student learning and the scholarship of teaching. Demonstrates how CATs can promote good teamwork in students, help institutions answer the call for program accountability, and guide new teachers in developing their teaching philosophies.
ISBN: 0-7879-9885-0

TL74 **Changing the Way We Grade Student Performance: Classroom Assessment and the New Learning Paradigm**
Rebecca S. Anderson, Bruce W. Speck
Offers alternative approaches to assessing student performance that are rooted in the belief that students should be active rather than passive learners. Explains how to use each assessment measure presented, including

developing criteria, integrating peer and self-assessment, and assigning grades.
ISBN: 0-7879-4278-2

TL73   **Academic Service Learning: A Pedagogy of Action and Reflection**
Robert A. Rhoads, Jeffrey P. F. Howard
Presents an academic conception of service learning, described as "a pedagogical model that intentionally integrates academic learning and relevant community service." Describes successful programs, and discusses issues that faculty and administrators must consider as they incorporate service learning into courses and curricula.
ISBN: 0-7879-4276-6

TL72   **Universal Challenges in Faculty Work: Fresh Perspectives from Around the World**
Patricia Cranton
Educators from around the world describe issues they face in their teaching practice. National differences are put into the context of universal themes, including responding to demands for social development and reacting to influences by government policies and financial constraints.
ISBN: 0-7879-3961-7

TL71   **Teaching and Learning at a Distance: What It Takes to Effectively Design, Deliver, and Evaluate Programs**
Thomas E. Cyrs
Offers insights from experienced practitioners into what is needed to make teaching and learning at a distance successful for everyone involved.
ISBN: 0-7879-9884-2

TL70   **Approaches to Teaching Non-Native English Speakers Across the Curriculum**
David L. Sigsbee, Bruce W. Speck, Bruce Maylath
Provides strategies that help students who are non-native users of English improve their writing and speaking skills in content-area courses. Considers the points of view of the students themselves and discusses their differing levels of intent about becoming proficient in English writing and speaking.
ISBN: 0-7879-9860-5

TL69   **Writing to Learn: Strategies for Assigning and Responding to Writing Across the Disciplines**
Mary Deane Sorcinelli, Peter Elbow
Presents strategies and philosophies about the way writing is learned, both in the context of a discipline and as an independent skill. Focusing primarily on the best ways to give feedback about written work, the authors describe a host of alternatives that have a solid foundation in research.
ISBN: 0-7879-9859-1

TL68   **Bringing Problem-Based Learning to Higher Education: Theory and Practice**
LuAnn Wilkerson, Wim H. Gijselaers
Describes the basics of problem-based learning, along with the variables that affect its success. Provides examples of its application in a wide range of disciplines, including medicine, business, education, engineering, mathematics, and the sciences.
ISBN: 0-7879-9934-2